Letters
from the Woods

Wishing you still mornings
among tall trees, hot coffee
in your cup, a fish on the
line, and a song in your
heart.

Michael C. Hurley

Letters
from the Woods

Looking at Life through the

Window of Wilderness

MICHAEL C. HURLEY

Ragbagger Publishing
Raleigh, NC

For Kip and Caroline,
to help them find their way.

Table of Contents

Author's Foreword   ix

Introduction   xiii

The Campfire—A Poem   xv

On Cochran's Pond   1

The Secret Life of Mud Daubers   7

A Question of Character   13

The Secret of Life   19

Northern Dreams   25

My Girl   31

Fear and Fear Itself   39

Paddling by Ear   45

A Dream of Spring   51

While Ye May   59

The Living Wilderness   63

Traveling Light   71

Memories of Maine   77

The Adventurous Life   83

The Simple Life   89

Original Wilderness Illustrations   95

The Kindness of Strangers   111

Return to Still Pond   119

'We Few, We Happy Few'   127

What, Me Worry?   133

On Solitude   141

Breaking Camp   149

A Perfect World   155

Time and Tide   161

A Young Man's Fancy   167

The Old Timers, The Old Times   173

Law and Wilderness   177

On Simplicity   185

Time, Speed & Distance   191

The Gypsy in Me   197

A Boy's Life   203

The View from Here   211

Index of Photographs   221

Author's Foreword

Letters from the Woods contains a collection of the essays I wrote between 1995 and 2003 for *Paddle & Portage*, a quarterly journal devoted to the lore and romance of canoe voyages in the North Woods tradition. This mode of travel was popularized in the eighteenth century by French-Canadian "voyageurs." They used the vast network of lakes and portage trails across Canada to bring fur pelts to Hudson Bay, where they would be loaded aboard ships for delivery to the fashion houses of Europe. The voyageurs would fish, paddle, portage and camp from lake to lake across vast distances, encountering a stunningly beautiful wilderness along the way. Their harsh but romantic way of life was the inspiration for modern-day voyageurs who paddle and camp along the rivers and lakes of North America for sport, relaxation, and adventure.

Each issue of the journal contained not only the contemplative essays you read in this book but narratives, photographs, and maps of far-flung trips that I enjoyed every year with family and friends. The trip narratives are not published, here, but you will notice references in some of the essays to "the story which appears in this issue." Only about a fourth of the photographs published in the journal appear in *Letters from the Woods*, but most of the illustrations are represented.

As explained somewhat in "The View from Here," the essay appearing in the final issue in Fall 2003, the growth and popularity of the journal came as a complete surprise to everyone, including me. I had by necessity become familiar with the workings of personal computers since opening a solo law practice in 1988. Having dabbled in freelance magazine and newspaper journalism in college, I was intrigued by the possibilities for "personal publishing" that came with the advent of the Windows operating system and more powerful desktop PCs, in the mid-nineties. Using a cheap, flatbed scanner for black-and-white photographs and the page-layout program that I had purchased to make brochures for my law practice, I was astonished that I could create a professional-looking magazine on my office laser printer. I named it "Hurley's Pack and Paddle," then later "Hurley's Journal," and printed it on ivory-colored, legal paper that was saddle-stitched and right-hand folded to make a bound volume. I sent copies to family and friends. One old friend in Houston, Dr. Mark Kunik, sent back a ten dollar bill and a note suggesting that I keep the issues coming. I decided to do just that.

During the infancy of the Internet, in December 1995, I patched together a marketing website for the journal with the help of the webmaster for the Wooden Canoe Heritage Association. I soon began to receive inquiries and subscriptions from website links and postings on canoeing newsgroups. Later, I discovered the Newsletter Publishers Association and learned how to create successful direct-mail campaigns. The journal expanded in size and content. After taking drawing classes at the Sertoma Arts Center in Raleigh, I gained enough confidence to create passable illustrations for the cover. A commercial offset printer took over production of the journal, and a mailing house began handling circulation and promotions. I adopted and trademarked the more marketable name, "Paddle & Portage." Freelance, regional editors began to take on some of the writing and traveling responsibility, but it became clear that my full-time law practice, which was growing just as quickly, would demand more of my schedule than my part-time publishing venture would allow. I also longed for more time to finish a novel, which is now underway. Although it was only a modest financial success, when I closed *Paddle & Portage* in January 2004, it had accumulated more than 10,000 subscribers in 48 states, Canada, and overseas during its eight-year run.

The highly personal, intimate style of the journal made readers seem more like close friends than customers. I used that intimacy and the editor's bully pulpit to say more to my readers than simply where to paddle and camp. Through these essays I wanted to express to them something of the hidden, eternal meaning of the wilderness through my experiences of it as a child and later as a husband and a father. As these stories unfolded with each new issue, the journal became less about canoeing and more about life.

To my surprise, the essays were the most popular feature of the journal and generated more reader mail than I had time to answer. The idea for this book was conceived by readers who asked that the complete essays be collected in a single volume, for others to enjoy. I am flattered to oblige these dear friends, and I hope that new readers will find the journey through these pages just as rewarding.

Michael C. Hurley
November 1, 2004

Introduction

All that is gold does not glitter,
Not all those who wander are lost.
The old that is strong does not wither,
Deep roots are not reached by frost.

— J. R. R. Tolkien, <u>Lord of the Rings</u>

Close your eyes and imagine traveling by canoe on a clear, autumn morning on a river in Maine. There you will find your gold in the abundantly beautiful leaves gently falling through the air just for you. Ah, nature's redeeming influence fills your soul and lifts you above the realities of life.

Letters from the Woods are the deep-rooted and passionate essays of a continued faith in wilderness and mankind that is so very much needed in the world today. In the era of SUV's, extreme-living, and theme parks it is comforting to know that there are still pockets in our world that are untouched and sacred ground just waiting to be paddled and wandered through.

Michael C. Hurley brings a human touch to the wilderness experience that conjures up a reflective and aesthetic emotion, making us feel as if we are part of the landscape of life. As in the essay "A Boy's Life," we realize the importance of nature in our lives and our family's lives as a revelation of our own existence.

Within the pages of this book you will laugh at the similarities all families share, cry at the most poignant moments in a young boy's adventures, and silently thank God for the honest and heartfelt tales of a man and his family as they travel by canoe to places many of us would not normally think to go.

I don't believe you can ever really finish a book like this without wanting or even needing to begin a journey yourself. Share these essays with your children and friends. When you are down and in need of a little inspiration, travel down the James River or the backwoods of Canada. Now is the time for family and friends to experience the close connection we have always had with each other and the wilderness. You may never own a canoe, but now you have an excuse for becoming a wanderer. Let the adventure begin.

Everyone must believe in something. I believe I'll go canoeing.
—Henry David Thoreau

The Campfire

A Poem

A weary dusk drifts down in silken mists,
and clouds float their burdens upon the tide.
A flame of white-hot birch defies the gloom with dancing fists,
but—alas—this fight must too subside.
It was ever thus, and will remain.
Sleep we all against the dawn,
our voyage to begin again.

On Cochran's Pond

Summer 2000

The door to the house was impressive if not a little intimidating. I had never come this far up the hill, before—all the way to the large, brick mansion that overlooked the patch of woods known to the kids in the apartments where I lived, nearby, as Cochran's Pond. I knew somehow that the people who lived here owned this land, where for the last five of my thirteen years I had dawdled and explored, played hooky and hockey and spent a goodly part of each day pretending this was a real wilderness—like the kind I had seen only in pictures—and not just a woodlot tucked within Baltimore's ever-growing suburbs.

Christopher Robin may have had his hundred-acre wood, and the Swiss Family Robinson their island, but I had Cochran's Pond. It was a place big enough for pretending. If you knew where to pick up the trail in the forest behind the neighborhood swimming pool, you

didn't need a key to get past the chain-link fence. In the summertime, it was just a short walk before you were completely hidden by the low branches of silver maple, white oak and hickory as you climbed the hillside above the pond. There was one tree in a clearing that must have been a variety of chestnut or hazelnut. I never could find the species in the field guide at the library, but its fruit made a tolerable meal for roasting over an open fire, whatever it was.

Higher on the hill, in the woods above the pond, fallen giants left hollow spaces in the ground, filled with the sweet smell and inviting "crunch" of leaves. As hiding places these were ideal. I would tuck myself in and sit for hours, waiting for the regular appearance of a red fox at dusk from his den in the earth beneath another fallen giant, just where the trees gave way to a small cow-pasture. Imagine, if you will, cows not three miles from the city and not eight miles from the stadium where Brooks Robinson played third base. I didn't have to imagine—it was real to me, with a real bull that chased me and my pals. We snuck inside the pen and waved our arms to see whether there was any truth to those cartoons about bulls and the color red. I remember how utterly unexpected it was when he came barreling at me. Charging, angry beasts were not everyday fare in these parts. I ran for all I was worth—getting that second leg above the top fence-rail not too very much ahead of the moment of pressing need that I do so. What an odd obituary it would have been, otherwise: "Baltimore boy trampled to death by raging bull behind apartment swimming-pool."

The woods of Cochran's Pond served as the backdrop for an array of boyhood adventures too numerous to recount—woodland and otherwise. There was bow-fishing for carp and the lessons on refracted light that I no longer remember. (Must one aim *below* the place where the fish appears to be, or is it *above*?) There was the other mansion—the haunted one that had fallen to ruins decades earlier and seemed to be littered as much with history as mystery. We boys had discovered the remains of a bowling alley among the creaking timbers of the basement. There wasn't much in life that seemed more unattainable to us at the time than having your own private bowling-alley, and finding it here only fanned the flames of imagination. But apart from these occasional trespassory episodes, the real attraction of the pond was the opportunity it offered to while away hours that might otherwise have been spent on schoolwork with my fingers dug into the mud, instead. I marked the first Earth Day in 1970 in solemn ceremony, here. I came to understand the

Mississippi Delta from the sand that the stream left where it settled into the pond. Most often, I looked at the waters of Cochran's Pond and imagined the lakes and woods of a faraway wilderness and the wild fish—the big ones—that lay hidden, there. I would have traveled to such places if I could, but the options open to a thirteen-year-old son of a single, working

mother being what they were, I resolved instead to make a sanctuary of Cochran's Pond. And so I stepped up to the door of that imposing mansion at the top of the hill, whose occupants did not know me from Huckleberry Finn nor I them, and knocked.

I knew I was out of my element when the butler met me at the door, though how I recognized his occupation I am not sure—he being the only butler I had ever seen. He greeted me, and the unexpected happened as it so regularly did in this enchanted forest. I was asked in to meet the master of the house, the courtly Mr. Merrick, and his wife. Before I knew it I was seated at a

formal dining table in my rumpled dungarees being offered—
I shall never, ever forget it as long as I live—a dinner of Lobster
Newburg.

In my memory the place was resplendent with Persian
rugs and had that smell of mahogany, leather and wool that, I
would later come to know, is so telling of Old Baltimore. I don't
recall the taste of the lobster or the homemade jam in little jars
sealed with wax, but I remember Mr. Merrick listening with
flattering interest to my plans to dredge Cochran's Pond and
stock it with bass—at his expense. What I lacked in funds I
made up in chutzpa.

The pond was silting in from street-water runoff that
came rushing down the creek, I explained (with studious
comparisons to the hydrology of the Mississippi Delta). I
proposed to take bids to dredge the bottom and oversee the
project. He agreed, and in a matter of a few months, one man
was reporting every day to operate a huge crane on the bank. In
the bucket would go and up it would come on a wire cable,
dumping its contents onto a growing moonscape of muck on
shore.

The dredging project took weeks to finish, and it all
must have seemed a little surreal to my grandmother. Fearing I
had perpetrated an expensive hoax, she intercepted a telephone
call from Mr. Merrick one morning to ask whether he was aware
that his foreman was only in 7th grade. He said that he was,
and he asked to speak to me. These were heady times for a
thirteen-year-old boy.

Mr. Merrick and his patch of woods entered my life only
briefly, but I was so much the better for it. The first "hard" job
I ever had was splitting logs for firewood, on his woodpile.
What I know of the simple art of building a campfire I
perfected, here. But there were larger lessons underway. Not

until I was much older did I appreciate the man who invited me in for dinner and took on my plan to save Cochran's Pond: Robert G. Merrick, Sr., a decorated veteran of World War I, a Ph.D. economist, a distinguished alumnus and benefactor of Johns Hopkins University, a scion of Wall Street, and for thirty-five years the president of Equitable Trust—one of Maryland's largest and most trusted banks.

Mr. Merrick is gone, now. Cochran's Pond has since been acquired by a nearby country club. The new owners have cleared part of the surrounding forest and encircled it with a more secure fence. Though I doubt many young interlopers will find a way in there to play, at least the pond lives on as a natural place of beauty. We are poorer today for the loss of other places like it.

As a nation we have done much to save the great open spaces, and it is well we should do more; but there is something special about the neighborhood woodlot. There is no pond in my children's neighborhood, and they have no secret woods. They have paddled and camped on more rivers than most men will see in their lifetimes, yet I miss for them that one patch of woods that they could know better than anyone—a place they could cherish and nurture for their own.

When I look back, now, I see what Mr. Merrick must have seen. I think of all the other paths a boy might have taken, and I am glad I took the one that led up a hillside beside a pond, where fallen giants had left hollow places for hiding, where the red fox came each day at dusk, and where life was sweet with the smell of leaves.

The Secret Life of Mud Daubers

Summer 1999

For this season's issue, I had long planned an opening essay on a lovely little pond and patch of woods that occupied a special corner of my boyhood. Then came the massacre at Littleton, Colorado, followed a month later by a similar attempt in Georgia. These events bring to me the palpable sense that at this time in our nation's history, reminisces on the lighter delights of a childhood spent outdoors are a sort of fiddling while Rome burns. I have even felt a tinge of guilt that, with the very fabric of society seeming to fray ever closer to the seam, the days we "grownups" spend relaxing in woodland camps are perhaps a little too self-indulgent. There's a war on for the hearts and minds of our children, and trivial pursuits are unbecoming of a people at war.

As I write these words I can hear the ready rejoinder of many of you that, had those boys in

Littleton only spent more time in the Great Outdoors than in
the darker alleys of the Internet, their hearts and minds would
have been drawn to high ideals. The sort of thinking in that
response is nothing new, of course, and I will be the first to
speak up for the many spiritual gifts imparted by a closeness to
the land. But the grotesqueness of what happened in Littleton
suggests to me that there is something amiss in our nation's life
that cuts far deeper than what songs around the campfire or any
number of miles washed down the wake of a canoe can heal.
The beauty of nature and the deprivations of camp living that
we cheerfully endure are a powerful therapy. They remind us of
the important things in life. But is that enough? Where do
we—and our children in particular—discover what the
important things are to begin with?

Last year I took my children to our state museum of
natural science and made just such a discovery. We had the
good fortune to stumble into a fascinating presentation, put on
by a talented curator who seemed to be enjoying his job greatly
out of proportion to what we, the taxpayers of North Carolina,

were paying him. He was unfolding a story for the enraptured children in the audience about the life of mud daubers—those wasp-like bugs that build clods of mud in organpipe formation in rafters and caves everywhere in the South.

It seems that the humble mud dauber is a rather busy and thoughtful fellow. In the earthen catacombs which it constructs it lays the eggs that will become the next generation of mud daubers, but it hardly leaves the fate of that generation to chance. A good deal of the mud dauber's day is spent accumulating a cache of spiders with which to feed its brood, and feed them in a rather strange and mysterious way. You see, the eggs take a fairly long time to hatch—at least in comparison to the shelf-life of dead spiders. If the adult mud dauber simply killed the spiders and stuffed them in the nursery like Twinkies in a lunchbox, they would decay too much to make a balanced, healthy diet by the time the babies were hatched. As the curator explained how the daubers get around this problem, his words made the hair on the back of my neck suddenly stand on end.

The adult mud daubers prevent the spiders from decomposing during the time it takes for gestation by catching them without killing them, then injecting them with exactly enough venom—not too much mind you, but just the right amount—to paralyze them. This ensures that the spiders will sit patiently still, helpless but very much alive, as they wait to become the hatchlings' first meal.

Three truths occurred to me from this story. The first of these, and what gave me the willies right off the bat, is that this rather sophisticated bit of engineering in food-storage science by mud daubers is no accident. It is possible to sing hymns and hallelujahs all one's life and never really come to terms with the awesome reality of a Creator, but often the greatest truths lie hidden in the smallest details. One cannot consider the attention God has paid to the proper care and feeding of the humble mud dauber and not shudder with the realization of what he must expect of us, whom he has made in his own image.

The second truth is born of pity for the poor spider. After all, the God who created the mud dauber also gave us Charlotte's Web and the clever engineer behind it. Do we suppose the life of mud daubers to be a cruel imposition on the life of spiders, and should we expect to find spiders railing against nature in anger or wandering in bewilderment as to the injustice of it all?

The truth evident in the spider's fate is that all life on Earth is temporary and incomplete. Whether one is a mud dauber, a spider or a king, the temporal world in the end does not offer a meaning for one's existence.

I have heard some in the media ask in vain, in the wake of the terrible events of this year, "why bad things happen to good people." There is a book by that title which I have not read, but the questioner's premise is that, in the natural order of things, health and well-being should reward the Good on this earth. The horrors of Littleton, therefore, necessarily represent a disturbance in that natural law. This way of thinking inevitably comes to grief in the death of an innocent child or a senseless accident. To seek a well-ordered justice in this world is an invitation to bitterness. Whether we find ourselves on the mean streets of the city or gazing at the moon from the shores of the wilderness, life all around us is brutal by nature.

There will always be those with romantic notions of human law and civilization, whose illusions about the power of politics and policy to shape behavior will be shattered in places like Littleton and Somalia and Rwanda. Better that we should find, in this parable of the mud dauber, a quiet reminder of our faith—a remembrance that we are only pilgrims in this land, placed here awhile for a particular purpose that is certainly not to rant at our own misfortune or to crave an illusory justice.

The third truth revealed in the mud dauber's lot is a lesson for parents. I was struck by the planning of which a tiny insect is capable to ensure the safety and survival of its offspring. It really is quite remarkable when you consider how many other ways a mud dauber might choose to spend its time. But when it comes to the question of what we humans should be doing to keep another schoolyard massacre from happening, don't expect to hear exhortations from me about gun control, the importance

of good schools, coaching your kids' soccer team, being a stay-at-home mom, V-chips, or any of the conventional wisdom. And don't expect me to tell you that if you make sure your kid grows up camping and canoeing with mom and dad, he'll never shoot up his school. This is where the analogy between men and mud daubers ends. Each one of these initiatives has its value, but ultimately our children's souls cannot be purchased at the paltry cost of a parent's time, better movies, or a well-planned and well-provisioned childhood.

I speak with some authority on this subject from my own experience. I grew up the happy child of a single mother who worked nights and weekends to make ends meet, and I was often home alone. I made not one camping trip with my father, for whom alcoholism was an ever-present reality. I attended public schools where drinking, drug-use and racial tension were neither rampant nor rare. Though I have no qualms about gun control, I was an enthusiastic hunter and spent my summers on a farm around enough firepower to kill every squirrel in the county, twice. One man's experience is not necessarily a lesson for all, but neither will I ignore what is obvious to me from my experience.

What was clear to me that day in Raleigh, as my children and I contemplated the secret life of mud daubers, is that there is a purpose to Creation. Knowing this, we are called by faith to enlist our lives in the service of that purpose. When we fail to heed that call, our lives turn down paths that are empty of lasting meaning—paths that lead to places like the tragedy at Columbine High. A life without faith is a life without hope. Children feel that lack of hope most acutely and are honest enough to dare to ask, "If this is all there is, why should I care?"

I realize that all of this may sound pretty corny to some, and my wife, who worries constantly about what each of you thinks of this journal, will chastise me for writing another homily. But make no mistake, Littleton was a clarion call to our nation. It poses a question that each of us fails to answer at his peril. We are called to remember that in the final analysis, life on this earth—with its pleasure and inevitable pain—is not about this earth. We may exult in the time we spend with our children and take them camping and fishing all over creation, but the enjoyment of these blessings is an aid to our faith, not the aim of our existence. May we and our children remember what elaborate plans God made for the life of mud daubers, and never despair or doubt what he has in store for us.

A Question
of Character

Spring 1998

T he rain, cold and fog were an inescapable state of affairs and had been so for days—long enough to dim the memory that there had ever been a sunny day or a balmy breeze on these waters. I was alone aboard the 28-foot sloop *Intrepid* on a broad reach into Pamlico Sound, an estuary so vast that European explorers first mistook it for another ocean. It was not a pleasure cruise. My appointed task was to deliver the boat to a berth twenty-five miles away in the coastal town of Oriental.

You could look at any point of the compass that December day and find no vision to relieve the gloom and gray. But there was one thing to be thankful for—a gentle, quartering breeze—were I inclined toward thankfulness at the time. I was not. Instead, I was underdressed for the weather, cold, and worried with good reason that I would not make the channel in sufficient daylight to stay off the shoals. The only thing that seemed possibly worse than sailing through this soup was spending the night aground in it. Then, slowly through the fog of my distemper came the bow of a little ship to port.

He passed close enough to speak, and through his yellow weathers I distinctly saw a smile. It was not the smile of a madman but of one who had learned how to smile when all impulses are to the contrary.

As he took my leave he lifted his mug to the rainclouds and remarked with wry enthusiasm, "What a great day!" I shouted my agreement without hesitation and meant it. His greeting had reminded me in an instant that, given all the things a human being could be doing on the planet at that moment, we were lucky men indeed. I sheeted in the jib and headed to weather.

The lesson shared between those boats in the fog will play out sooner or later in every endeavor of our lives and is one we never master. For those of us who journey through wild places by canoe, it is a lesson we have the privilege to practice almost daily.

Companions suspect it may be some particular disfavor I have engendered with the gods, but whatever the reason, rare is the journey I make that is not attended by its own special tests of character. An extended canoe-trip compresses in time and space much of the epic of life. We plan, study and equip ourselves for a passage to unknown places. To succeed in this passage we must summon the resolve at each new landing in the forest to construct a shelter, gather fuel for warmth, secure our provisions against predation by wild beasts and the elements, and plan for the journey ahead. A team of voyagers as any other group must constitute and obey some hierarchical system of government, and those charged with governance of the voyage must judge wisely or subject the entire company to dire and immediate consequences. We may think it is just another canoe trip, but in these daily rituals we repeat a liturgy that is at the very foundation of every successful civilization in history. The driving spiritual force at the heart of that liturgy—the strength of which will ultimately foretell the success or failure of the venture—is character.

Character is nothing less than the gift to experience the present reality not as a moment fixed in time but as part of a larger and more complex whole. Character is that faithful remembrance of the past and unshakable confidence in the future that sustains us through the deprivations of the present. It matters little where or how tests of character come, the mettle required is always the same. The ability to look past the occasional deficits of a marriage and see the value appreciating over the long term is the same ability which compels us to add one paddle stroke to the next, even when it seems that the sum of our efforts will be too little, too late to purchase our goal against the surcharge of wind, weather and fatigue.

There have been many times—more than I care to recall nor would have space in this journal to recount—when life has presented me with a bill that I had insufficient funds of character with which to pay. That I preferred my personal pleasure over volunteering to serve my country as a younger man is chief among a myriad of errors of omission whose reparation now forever eludes me. But in looking back at every instance in which we are put to the test, the conflict is always the same: The temptation to despair and fly from a present, certain duty strains against the will to persevere toward a future, unseen goal. Would that God had granted us the ability to see the future, but thanks be given for the gift of character to guide us in its stead.

I did not set out to make wilderness canoeing a salve for my spiritual angst or a regimen for personal improvement. My reasons were much more banal: It was the fishing. Yet I cannot help but notice the character-building effect of these journeys. Indeed, in the work-a-day world carried on largely within air conditioned offices and upon cushioned furniture, I would soon lose my bearings if I did not regularly retreat to a place where life is reduced to its fundamentals.

One of my more formative lessons in the fundamentals of life came one summer in the Adirondacks. I was alone on the first leg of a ninety-mile journey from Old Forge to the town of Saranac Lake that was expected to last eight days. It seemed that the heavens had reserved the entire world's allotment of rain to follow me through those woods. The carry from Eighth Lake to Browns Tract Inlet was thick with mosquitoes and seemed interminable. As, discouraged and tired, I shoved the bow of my canoe through the dusk into Raquette Lake, the sky opened again—with an added insult of lightning. That night I shirked the usual duties of an evening in camp and crawled into my tent to brood. The next day, I packed up and paddled to the nearest road, caught a ride back to my car, and drove home. None would blame me. The awful weather was expected to continue for days.

After returning home, a strange sense of remorse came over me. The sun eventually came out, and tired muscles soon recovered, but I was not happy to be in the comfort and warmth of my living room. I wanted to be back at that rain-soaked camp in the Adirondacks—back at that moment in time when I still had a chance to look a fight in the eye with fists raised and say "Try me!" But it was too late. The water was under the bridge, and other duties intruded. The memory of that regret chiseled this rule into my wilderness lectionary: Once begun, never turn from a journey to follow your ease.

Some say we remember discontented days in the woods more fondly in hindsight because we choose to forget our pain. I disagree. It is not that we fail to recall hardship, rather only that with the passage of time it occupies a rightly smaller place in the larger landscape of life's joys. Character is simply the vision to see that landscape through the fog of the moment and say, with conviction, "What a great day!"

The Secret of Life

Fall 2000

I t is no small sign of the fundamental goodness of mankind that utter strangers sit quietly by when I play the guitar in public places. Yes, our friends, neighbors, and all but the most determined passersby now surely know that the classical guitar is my newfound obsession. A Christmas gift from my wife almost two years ago, in the time since it has carved out that space in my evening hours that formerly belonged to the glowing, blue tube in our living room. It has rekindled my interest in music that began on the piano, thirty years ago. My son the violin player has taken on the guitar as a second instrument. Both children and I are accomplices in a nightly conspiracy to push the envelope of bedtime: They know that the last inkling of the day can be postponed almost indefinitely by asking Daddy, who waits expectantly at the foot of the bed with guitar in hand, to play "Mamas, Don't Let Your Babies Grow Up to Be Cowboys" one more time.

People may suspect that Willie Nelson can't really sing, but there's no doubt at all about me. So, it was especially heartwarming that at this summer's rendezvous in the Adirondacks, the band of paddlers assembled for the last night around the campfire let me howl on in good measure. To their credit, a few even crooned along for a few bars of "Puff, the Magic Dragon," the "Garden Song" and "What a Day for a Daydream." It was great fun—for me, at least, and if not for others they were kind enough not to show it.

Driving home from the rendezvous through the mountains of Pennsylvania, I was listening to the country station as I am now wont to do, always looking for new material. A song came on the radio that I had heard before, but the words struck me differently, this time. You may have heard it yourself. Sung by Faith Hill, it is entitled "The Secret of Life"—and what a melancholy treatment of the subject it is.

As the song goes, the nightly ritual of a couple of regulars at the "Starlight Bar" is interrupted when one of them laments the pointlessness of their life of "workin' and drinkin' and dreams." This leads to a chorus of metaphors such as one might imagine would be offered up by his bar chums at just such moments of introspection. Before the song is over, the secret of life is said variously to be found in a good cup of coffee, Monday Night Football, the inviting gaze of Marilyn Monroe, a well-made martini, getting up early, staying up late, and so on in a series of banalities. Ultimately, despondently, the singer tells us that "The secret of life is there aint no secret, and you don't get your money back." It just goes to show you what a rough day in the saddle can do to a songwriter's mental attitude.

As for me—I thought smugly as I drove along—I had certainly found the secret of life. After all, unlike all those poor devils back in Raleigh, working themselves to death in the drudgery of full-time law practice, I had chosen to absent

20

myself from the partnership track to devote more to time to enjoying life—time I have spent paddling all over this country, writing this journal, and, lately, learning classical guitar.

In my self-satisfaction, I recalled the sad story of a well-known and very successful attorney who found himself terminally ill at a young age. When I heard that his final words were of regret for never having made a trip that he and his young son had long dreamed of taking together, I mentally crossed that one off of my own list of possible regrets. Name a state, name a river, and there's a fair chance my kids and I have been there in a canoe. Come to think of it, I could now cross off learning a new musical instrument from my list of "things to do before I die." "Yessiree," I told myself. "I'm a heck of a lot smarter than all those money grubbers who haven't figured out that it isn't the guy who dies with the most toys who wins—it's the guy who makes the best use of his leisure time." Isn't that right? And don't you readers of this journal know this same secret: getting out to enjoy God's creation while you still can, as often as you can, and soaking in all the beauty of the world? Whether it be canoeing, saving the whales, surfing the eddies, golfing, or what-have-you, find your thing in life and do it to the hilt. Isn't that what life is all about?

Well, actually—no. To tell you the truth, I met the secret of life when I was very young. She was a child at a home for sick children in Baltimore that our youth group visited one Christmas when I was about sixteen. She had a rare disease that withered the skin from her face so that she appeared literally to be a skeleton. It required a conscious effort on my part just to look at her, but she was as happy and as talkative and as wrapped up in the coming of Christmas as any child I ever met.

In that child's smile I knew even then that I had found the secret of life, but in the years that followed I was certain that if I looked hard enough I could find that secret in other places more pleasing to the senses—in the right woman, in enough knowledge, in a brilliant career, in hard work and a nice home and a comfortable salary, and—yes—beside a campfire, under the stars, in a woods one can reach only by the silent thoroughfares of the canoe. But the secret of life is no more to be found in those places than in a country song.

Let me tell you the secret of life, friends. I certainly make no claim to the discovery of this knowledge—I am only happy to possess it. It makes for uninteresting copy in this Enlightened Age, but it is, I assure you, the bona fide secret if you can accept it. No, it is not the dip of a well-turned paddle or the call of a loon. It is not the smell of balsam or the dancing light of a campfire. It is only this, and nothing more: That we should love God with all of our heart and mind and soul, and love our neighbor as ourselves. Study that line once more. It's old news, but good news just the same. What does it mean?

Some of you, I know, are reading this and asking why I cannot just stick to paddling and leave the Almighty out of it. That is, of course, the Great Lie of our times—that we shall have a civil society apart from God.   It is not just freedom *of* religion, but freedom *from* religion that so many in our nation now seek. We have already begun to see the fruits of that lie in places like Columbine and pop idols like Eminem. After all, if the only moderating influence in our civic life is no longer a divine imperative, if we make a diety of our free will and a dogma of our pleasure, who is to say that one man's diety won't be another man's death, or that one man's pleasure won't be another man's pain? Take a trip to your local movie theater sometime, and you'll get a good idea of how the experiment is going so far. The ideals that make for a civil society—kindness, compassion, self-sacrifice—are anchored in the faith that there is a purpose and a recompense to life on Earth that is greater than our collective quest for personal satisfaction while we are here.

It is well that we should repair to the wilderness to refresh our minds and bodies, and there the beauty of life we shall surely find. But the secret of life, life's very goal, is closer at hand. The love of neighbor is not just a warm welcome to our

friends but a hand stretched out to our enemies. It is food to a hungry and undeserving stranger, clothing to a poor and illegal immigrant, and a life lived in service of a purpose broader than our own families.

Imagine, if you will, that we have been put on this earth to accomplish only this and nothing more in our days, here: To love and obey God, and to love and serve our neighbor as ourselves. Imagine that all creation redounds to those two objectives. Imagine that, and do me this favor: Find me twenty years from today, and ask not how many rivers I have paddled, but how well I have kept the secret of life.

Northern Dreams

Summer 1997

I t had seemed a long drive from suburban Baltimore to Deer Creek, the "designated trout stream" where, my father had somehow learned, the fishing was fast and furious. Along the way we stopped at a tackle shop to purchase a bamboo fishing pole—my first—that came with an impossibly large bobber and braided line of the type in wide use before the advent of monofilament. I was nine or ten years old. Except for a few, blurry flashes of earlier memory, it was the first outing with Dad that I can recall.

Sons of absent, alcoholic fathers will understand too well the hope and unease that surrounds such reunions. Without the usual, day-to-day exchange between parent and child to define for me who and what my father was, he became in my mind an amalgam of the stories—part truth, part fancy—told by and about him. Those stories often revolved around the culture

which he and his
brothers shared with
other families of Irish
ancestry who found
success in large cities
early in this century.
There were whispers of
the money his father had
made and somehow lost
as an executive in the
canning business. There
were stories of the

privileged youth he and his brothers spent in private schools and
summers at Indian Lake; of his brother's 42-foot wooden
sailboat, *Cygnet*, the Larchmont Yacht Club, and a garment
business with offices in the Empire State Building; of his college
days at Columbia and nights spent busing tables for the glitterati
at the 21 Club; of the letter of acceptance from Harvard Law
School that went unanswered because his father's money had run
out; and, finally, there were those stories held in common with a
nation of that long, dark tunnel called World War II.

After he was tested at the Battle of Peleliu and other
venues of the U. S. Marines in the South Pacific, the stories
which followed my father were mostly about the drinking. But
hope springs eternal in a young boy clutching his first fishing
pole on a brisk march through the tall grass to his first trout
stream, and the stories I chose to remember then were about the
Adirondacks.

I doubt I knew where or what the Adirondacks were, at
my age, beyond the image of a vaunted, shining wilderness filled
with fish, game, and fresh air. My father called this place
repeatedly to mind, however, in contrast to the place where we
happened to be. The trout fishing on Deer Creek by the time
we arrived, several days after the spring opener, was neither fast

nor furious. Some locals finally explained to my father the routine: Hatchery trout are no sooner poured from buckets upstream than they are ignominiously hoisted from the water on bait of kernel corn by hordes of fishermen crowded along the downstream shoreline.

When my father and I arrived, there were no other fishermen and, it soon seemed apparent, no fish. Nonetheless, Dad schooled me in the proper technique. Creeping cautiously up to the bank and shushing me to make no noise, he directed my cast toward a likely looking pool. Nothing. Another pool,

another cast, and again, nothing. And so it went for the afternoon until the fishing fell into reminisces about days he and his brothers spent bushwhacking along little streams in the Adirondacks. "If there were a fish in there," he would say, "as soon as your fly hit the water— POW!" I was eager for the "pow" part to begin, but as it turned out my first fish would be not nearly so lofty as a native Adirondack brook trout.

Hillary Sullivan and I were the kind of friends known only to the Neverland of

boyhood. But of all the adventures, schemes, and misdemeanors we shared, rising at dawn to pursue the carp of Lake Roland was not to be one of them. Hillary rolled over when the alarm went off, but I got rigged and ready. Carrying the same unlucky bamboo pole from my father and a bag of dough balls concocted of white bread, vanilla extract, molasses, and sugar, I set out for glory. It was a testament to my disbelief that I carried nothing with me in which to keep a fish if I actually caught one.

The sun rose over the lake while I patiently stared at my bobber ten feet out from a well-worn spot on shore. A man passed by and, asking what I was after, commented that a carp would break my pole when I caught one. That seemed a little over the top to me at the time, given that I'd never caught a fish, much less one capable of any such destruction. Not ten minutes later, however, my bobber shot south. I reared back on the skittering bamboo pole, which promptly split down its length and became as limp as a blade of grass. Others might have taken that cue to surrender, but I had something to prove. Wallowing waist deep into the cold water of early spring, I snatched the broken tip of my pole as it was being towed out to sea. Then, stumbling and sloshing backwards toward shore, with the bare line in my hand, I soon had a fat, two-pound carp flipping on the ground at my feet. Winning the lottery could scarcely compare to my sense of incredible luck and euphoria at that moment. It was not a trout nor even a bass, but I walked two miles back to Hillary's house with that trophy clasped to my chest. When I called my father for instructions on how to clean and cook a carp, he responded with an old saw: "Boil it for two hours in a pot filled with water and a large rock, then eat the rock." And while even I appreciated the wisdom of that recipe after the bony dish was served, to his credit Dad joined me in the feast.

After those days I encountered other fruitless, well-trodden streams, but occasionally there would be that experience which seemed to recall the mythic promise of the northlands. It was those experiences, like the time-worn stories of my father's glory days, that I chose to remember. Those higher hopes, not the failures and the disappointments, were always brought to the fore as each new adventure was planned.

In the spring of this year, now five seasons since my father's death, I finally reached the headwaters of the legendary Oswegatchie River—a proving ground of trout fishermen in decades past. Whether my father ever walked these virgin woods it is too late to ask, but doubtless he saw others like them. There, deep in the heart of this most primal region of the Adirondacks, I crept quietly upon a rock below High Falls.

Spotting a likely looking pool, I cast my lure. No sooner had I turned the handle of my reel, when—POW! An exquisite specimen of the famed Adirondack brook trout, not more than 8 inches long, was wriggling at the end of my line. I eased it back into the river, there to grow not nearly so fast as it will in my memory. For what I choose to recall of this and every trip is neither the size nor the number of fish, neither the pain of the portage nor the chill of the wind, neither the luckless days nor the cloudy skies, but rather that vaunted, shining wilderness which is every sportsman's highest ideal and dearest dream.

My Girl

Fall 1998

In the heat of a Virginia summer, as we lay beneath a canopy of leaves on a ridge in the Shenandoah Mountains, the two of us heard the noise begin slowly. It started as just a distant rustling of the brush in the early morning, long before dawn, but became steadily, unmistakably closer. We either had no tent or had chosen not to pitch it in the sweat and swelter—I cannot remember now, seventeen years hence. But given what little we did have in the first months of our marriage, it would not surprise me to recall that we were just doing without.

We had certainly done without the night before. After borrowing my sister's VW wagon to make the trek from our apartment in Maryland for a "honeymoon" weekend of backpacking in Shenandoah National Park, we had arrived in Front Royal too late to hit the trail. A cheap hotel would have to do.

Were it not for the innkeeper's taxidermy displays that recalled Hitchcock's *Psycho* too vividly in Julie's mind, we would have had better sense than to walk away from the last vacant room in town. After whiling away another hour of fruitless searching, Julie relented and we returned to ask Mr. Bates for the room—only to find that one gone, too.

The back of a VW wagon is not quite 5'10" long, but I am. And getting married was supposed to mean never again

 having to say "Gee, honey, this parking lot looks dark enough," but we did that night. My plan, if the Hardee's manager came out to complain about our being parked there too long, was to tell him in no uncertain terms that Julie's father was the executive vice president of the company (true) and that she had the pull to have a mere store manager summarily dismissed if he didn't back off and leave us alone (not even close to true). Thankfully, I never had to explain to the manager of that Front Royal Hardee's—or to my wife, for that matter—why we were sleeping in a borrowed VW in the parking lot of a hamburger stand, in the first place.

The long answer to that question is still in the rough-draft stage, but the short answer was, "the money." Young, fearless, and high on the challenge of making a life together, we were determined to starve our own way. We had held onto hope against hope for a honeymoon at a cottage in the Adirondacks, that summer, but we just couldn't swing it. I still have the now-tattered brochure that shows an aerial photo of Raquette Lake amid a carpet of woods spreading out for miles. The little cottage in another picture, set back in the trees on Pine Island, seemed as quaint as you might imagine. I don't know why the owner didn't tell us it was our tough luck for canceling our reservation so late in the season, but we were more glad than he could know to have our deposit back.

When dawn came, we fired up the VW with the $39 Earl Scheib paint job (Gatorade green) and sputtered away before the breakfast crew got suspicious. At the park gate, the ranger gave us the scare report about lions, tigers and bears, which we blithely ignored. By mid morning, we were already deep in the woods, casting for trout with a fishing rod I had given Julie for her 21st birthday. (Yes, I was an incurable romantic even then.)

It is easier to get lost on foot in the woods than in a canoe on a lake where, sooner or later, one will bump into the shore. The lesser-used trails we had chosen (of course) were overgrown and hard to follow. More than once I humored Julie in her insistence about which way to go to regain our bearings, only to come to the unspoken realization that she had been right all along. Everything I needed to know about married life was revealed to me in the woods that weekend, slow though it has been to sink in.

What rare spasm of forethought had prompted me to hang our pack from a tree that night, I am not sure. At the age of 23 I planned for few things in advance. We were well off the trail in a hardwood forest, sleeping on a bed of dry leaves, when the noise in the blackness changed unmistakably to footsteps. I was no Daniel Boone, but my subconscious mind apparently could not reconcile the pace and rhythm of the noise with the usual motions of the night forest. When my deductive powers finally stumbled to the conclusion that this was indeed

the sound of four heavy legs, I woke up. My arm shot out and pinned Julie to the forest floor beside me. She was so very pleased to be there at the time, as I recall.

Exactly how the sacrament of marriage imparts to the union of two people a strength greater than the sum of their fears is one of the mysteries of Faith. Many, many times since that summer have I reached out and found uncommon courage to face life's twists and turns in the simple gesture of touch between a man and wife. It also helps to hang your food pack in a tree.

Apparently finding nothing to eat but the two stiff, moribund creatures on the forest floor—and they thankfully not to his liking—the beast wandered off. In the morning we found our way out of the woods in time to save fond memories of the experience; the VW started on the first crank; and we began the

ride home listening to the radio play the John Denver tune, "Some Days Are Diamonds, Some Days Are Stone." So it has been these seventeen years, much more for the better than the worse.

Just a few months ago a letter arrived from a concerned reader who hoped that the absence of my wife from many of the stories in this journal was not a sign of a decline in "friendly relations" between us. I bounded down the stairs from our home office to show the letter to Julie, who responded with characteristic bemusement. Having known me "when," she waits expectantly for the day when all of the present 5,000 readers of this journal will realize that I haven't the foggiest idea of what I am talking about and I am forced to slip quietly into a life of gardening and bridge.

But the reader's letter was an occasion for some reflection, as reader letters often are. I realize that many men have the company of their wives on trips into the wild. Is it a sign of some disaffection that I usually do not? I shouldn't think so. The reason has something to do with our basic assumptions about the individual in married life.

What I have learned about marriage after seventeen years could have saved us a lot of the usual arguments and frustrations at the outset of that journey. It is a lesson I dare say that men—being self-absorbed by nature—are more in need of learning than women. Yes, it would please me greatly if Julie joined me whenever I went into the field. A photo on a recent cover of a men's magazine showing a comely young woman in a bikini, pulling a canoe through the marsh while her beau reclines in the stern, captured this fantasy quite nicely. (Wives everywhere, please take note.) What I enjoy most, though, are those long, where-will-life-take-us conversations around the campfire. That's what makes a trip meaningful to me. But the elusive truth is that marriage is not about "me" or my personal satisfaction and never was. The object of the game is not my happiness or contentment—these are fringe benefits earned in the pursuit of a simpler but much loftier goal. That goal is the survival and success of the union itself.

A pastor whom I greatly admire once observed that, in our narcissistic culture, we err by filtering the question of whether, when or how to obey God through our own myopic, mortal sense of what will bring us joy and contentment. We've got it exactly backwards. Joy and contentment, he would teach us, flow from an obedience to God if for no better reason than that He is God and we are not. What a profoundly repugnant notion that is, in a country which venerates the individual, self-determination, and personal freedom increasingly above all else, and where the "Me Generation" reigns supreme.

Two people are at first drawn to each other by physical attraction and the sense of personal affirmation that each derives from the other's companionship. We could hang together for scarcely ten minutes in the absence of these adhesives, but they make a poor mortar with which to build a life together. There will always be someone else who is more attractive, and Mr. or Ms. Right will eventually tire of the job of assuring our continual aggrandizement. Over the long haul, there will come a cold, sober moment when all that separates us from the abyss of self-indulgence is the power of the promise we have made to each other. From our commitment to obey the promise in that moment—if for no better reason than because it is a promise—comes a wife's trust and the sound sleep of little children. From that trust comes the freedom to celebrate each other's differences without fear of being divided by them. And in that freedom abides the peace, joy and contentment we have been searching for all long.

Fear and Fear Itself

Winter 1997

On a gray July afternoon, the waning daylight made silhouettes of a party of canoeists struggling to make headway against the Canadian wind. It was a north wind, for which Lake Opeongo is duly famous. We watched them from the warmth of our campfire, sheltered from the blow beneath a knoll of granite and moss. The smell of fresh, baked bread and cedar smoke wafted through the air. It was a good day to be in camp, and the youngsters in the approaching canoes knew that as well as anyone.

They were a group of a dozen boys, all about thirteen years of age, accompanied by two Toronto teachers working as counselors at a summer camp. For the last mile they had hunkered in the lee of the point of land on which we were camped, finding there some respite from the boarding waves in unprotected water. To our pleasant surprise, they chose not to round the point into the teeth of the wind but instead pulled into camp on the leeward shore. Apologies for the intrusion and assurances that they would stop only for a moment were cheerfully interrupted by an invitation to stay the night. They thanked us but deferred their answer, while their eyes moved from the map, to the lowering north sky, to the mound of split wood beside our campfire, then back to the map. Meanwhile, my son Kip and his cousin Bennett, at seven years apiece, were electrified into action by the arrival of the older boys. Various shells, bugs, and rope projects were retrieved from around camp and presented to the bewildered guests for inspection and approval. Bennett's father and I roused the fire a little higher while the young campers eagerly succumbed to offers of brownies and bread with jam. Wet jackets were hung on the clothesline, and soon every hand held a steaming mug of spiced cider. The leaders finally concluded that it was pointless to resist further and joined us for the night.

Later that evening, while the younger campers attended to roasting marshmallows, the leaders discussed with us their plans and the glories of living so close to such a boundless wilderness. "Did you hear of the bear attack in the North Arm two weeks ago?" they asked. We had not. The ranger had mentioned only that there had been some "bear problems" in the North Arm and told us to be sure to hang our food at night. I thought it strange that she marked in large, black letters across our permit, "Advised about bears," but precautions against food-pack raiders of all stripes were already part of our routine.

The men explained that the incident involved a group of boys from another summer camp in the area who were making their annual canoe-trip through Lake Opeongo into the interior of Algonquin Park. They had placed their food in canoes and moored the canoes out in the lake, to avoid bear problems. At about two o'clock in the morning, a bear came into the camp where an eleven-year old boy from Montreal and two other

children were sleeping in one of the group's several tents. The bear reportedly tore into the tent and began to drag the boy off by the foot. An intrepid counselor who heard the screaming smashed one canoe paddle over the bear's head, then bludgeoned it with a second paddle until it ran up a tree.

The counselors put the boy in a canoe and took him to a nearby campsite where a motorboat could be seen. He was rushed to the ranger station, and a call for help was made. According to a report in the *Toronto Star*, the boy will recover fully. Rangers confirmed that there was no food at the site where the bear attacked and could not explain the bear's behavior. They later found and shot a bear that they determined by the paddle marks on its skull had committed the attack. It was reported to be a healthy, normal animal.

Well, this certainly was food for thought as we contemplated retiring in the woods that evening. Still, I reasoned, we were at least four miles from the location of the attack. Then our guests began with the next, more horrible story:

"A lot of folks camp on islands out here thinking they're safe from the bears," they explained. "But six years ago, a man and a woman were found cached on Bates Island ["cache" being the word for a carcass which a bear has buried for a future meal]." Bates Island is a beautiful spot not more than a twenty-minute paddle from the ranger station. Kip had begged me to make camp there on our way out, but there was little firewood, and it is a busy spot; the island forms a bottleneck through which all traffic heading back to the road must pass. It seemed an unlikely place for a bear attack.

There are many things to fear in a canoe trip, but seldom have my thoughts been pre-occupied with the risk of bears. I have long understood the importance of securing the food well up and away from the tent—chipmunks and raccoons are a ravenous bunch. But those things which I fear most relate to the safety of my children in the elements. Indeed, the sole consolation of a canoe trip without Kip—my even-keeled, ever-ready companion—is the leave which his absence grants to confront every rapid and squall with giddy abandon. A crossing with my wife and children is fraught with unspoken concern for my plan should the canoe become swamped in open water. Behind every sunny sky that heralds the departure of laughing children is a blackening storm that threatens disaster for their return. But still we go, because somehow we understand that a life without risks is a life not worth living. A child sheltered from all of life's dangers is one who will know few of its joys.

People who consider that in writing this journal I am living in the woods some two months out of the year often ask whether I carry a weapon for safety against black bears. I do not. The risk is too great that my wife, in a fit of sleep dementia, would take me for Sasquatch on my return trip from the loo and blow me to kingdom-come before the first bear ever showed up. To be truly effective in a moment of urgent need, the gun would have to be left loaded in the tent at night, and loaded guns don't belong on canoe trips with kids. Despite the tragic exceptions, the real risk of encountering a predacious black bear in one's tent at night is small—Field & Stream has yet to recommend retiring to a tent with a gun in its annual issue on bear-hunting techniques.

Still, a father worries about his children. As I settled into our tent in the Canadian woods that night in July, I vowed that it will be an unfortunate bear that ever attempts to drag away a child of mine. But the better part of valor knows that a father cannot protect his child from every danger—animal or otherwise. Like the reassurance that FDR once gave a nation, more often the greater danger in the woods comes not from that which we fear but from the paralysis of fear itself. Pity the child who is never allowed the chance to face life's bogeymen and overcome them. With that in mind, I drifted off to a peaceful sleep.

Paddling by Ear

Summer 1998

Amid the cobblestone streets of Baltimore's Mount Vernon section, where statues of our Founding Fathers festooned with pigeons have watched a century pass, the gargoyles guarding the entrance to the Peabody Conservatory of Music have watched along with them. Some thirty years ago they bit their tongues as a distracted young man passed those portals each week en route to a ritualized agony of childhood known as "piano lessons."

Actually, I loved the piano—still do. I picked out the notes of my first songs by ear on an instrument purchased for my sister Suzie and by third grade had learned a three-chord boogie-woogie well enough to be lead piano-banger in a trio of pals. At an early age I rarely missed tuning in to the Harley Show on AM radio at night to hear the riffs and rhythms of Oscar Peterson, Earl "Fatha" Hines, Fats Waller, and all the greats.

At 18, I was the only male student at Western Maryland College with his own key to the women's dormitory, where a concert-size grand piano beckoned me decidedly more often than the women did. I could hum more standards than Steely Dan tunes, was a fixture at sorority wine-and-cheese parties, and even did a stint for cash at Cockey's Tavern, but Peabody wasn't interested in any of it. Peabody was a place of notation and theory, of tempo, timbre and timing—of playing a piece exactly the way Bach wrote it and jolly well liking it, thank you. It was, ultimately, a place to which I was politely asked not to return after the exasperation proved too much for my instructors.

I used to waste time wondering what might have been "had I only applied myself," but one of the benefits of the passing years is that a pattern of this behavior eventually emerges—and, along with it, the means to rationalize most of life's left turns under the notion of "larger forces at work." In my case, those forces were at war against conformity, obedience, deference to authority, and many other core values of a well-ordered society. Their armies have been winning most of the skirmishes if not the war in my life, and this journal is among the spoils. By whose leave, after all, does an improbable voyageur from the suburbs of Baltimore presume to write "The Quarterly Journal of Traditional Canoe Camping"?

By whose leave, indeed. Giants have stalked the North Woods before us all—Bill Riviere, Sigurd Olson, and Bill Mason to name a few of the latter-day saints. I have read but hardly studied their works, and I knew none of them. More to the point, I have carefully avoided following too closely any one man's particular approach to journeying in the wilderness—not that I wouldn't do well by a closer study of the masters, mind you. I simply believe that life is best lived at your own risk—as a process of creative error and rediscovery, not a calculated imitation of what has gone before.

In fact, I get a subtle sense of unease whenever I read someone else's idea of how, exactly, to negotiate a difficult piece of whitewater—as if it might deprive me of the satisfaction of taking credit for my own accomplishments. Some gain real benefit from careful study of proper form, but there are those of us who are hard-wired to extemporize everything in life. After all, what fun is there in going bleary-eyed trying to learn paddling maneuvers such as cross-braces and draws from confusing diagrams, when a sense of "what to do next" ultimately must come to you (or not) like an epiphany in the middle of a real set of rapids? I may have flirted with *Study and Planning*, but *Necessity*—and more often her sister *Dire Necessity*—have been the mothers of my inventions. That's why you will never see an article in this journal presuming to teach you the dance steps you'll need to go lightly over your next waterfall.

There is ample opportunity nowadays to get caught up in notions of the "right way" and "wrong way" of doing things in

the wild. I remember a man who climbed into the bow of my canoe for a short paddle across a riffles to an island in the river, where we planned to saw up a boatload of driftwood for our fire. He had recently been to a high-flown paddling school—one of those places where kids in trick boats and wetsuits teach the "sport" of paddling to well-heeled suburbanites eager to catch on to the Next Big Thing. No sooner had we eased into the current than he became a tornado of activity, punching the water with his paddle on one side and then the other, angled this way and that way, in short bursts of surgical precision. You would have thought we were in the Olympic trials and that Hell Falls loomed just ahead. It was exhausting just watching him. I had never known how much difficult and complex work I had been missing in the simple task of moving from point A to point B. For the rest of the trip I was sure I looked like a sloth on a barge.

A similar experience occurred when some friends first invited me up to their favorite river for an overnighter. These were students of the Old School. They had a curious paddling style I had not seen before but have since come to recognize as the North Woods stroke popularized by Bill Mason. Mason was to the Canadian canoeing tradition what Mickey Mantle was to baseball. Kids practiced swinging like Mickey, and wilderness-seekers everywhere still want to do most things as Mason did them. Clinics are regularly held at canoeing festivals to teach the North Woods paddling style, and those who claim to have mastered it swear by it. Most of the hotshots in the wilderness-canoeing biz paddle this way. You'll notice ads in canoeing magazines with paddlers posed in the turned-down-wrist finish that is characteristic of Mason's style. It's a fine style, at that.

No sooner had I started out on the trip with these fellows than I noticed that they had stopped ahead and were staring back as I came down the river. I began to feel like the only man in a sport coat at a black-tie affair. What they were watching was the way the editor of a journal of traditional canoe-camping paddled his canoe. What they were seeing was not  Mason but a modified feather-stroke from the Boy Scout Handbook, with a little English thrown in. It is an ungainly sight, to be sure, but I can paddle in that groove from sunup to sundown, day after day, and never miss a beat. They tried to teach me the North Woods stroke, but I proved to be an incorrigible Old Dog.

Here's the lesson, friends: When you listen to a cut of Oscar Peterson taking off for the stratosphere at the Blue Note, you know he's playing it the way he feels it—the way that no one, including Oscar himself, has ever played that piece before. That's his gift. You can't deconstruct it, you can't teach it, and you can't recreate it from a page of sheet music. You've got to feel it. "Feeling it" is all that you can really learn from any master. No one ever painted a Renoir by the numbers, and the art of the wilderness is not in how well you travel, but why. The great tradition to which this journal aspires is not a set of techniques to be memorized or gear to be accumulated. It is the freedom of every man to write his own opus across the tattered pages of the woods and play it as far and long as his imagination will carry him.

A Dream of Spring

Fall 2002

"Ah, Fall." We say those words with bitter-sweetness, as a father speaks the name of a wayward child who grew up and left him too soon. Only yesterday our world was sultry and serene, but now we are left to our early evenings beside the fire, sipping something warm and growing weary with regret for the lost love that was Summer.

Our journey through the seasons began with the first, tentative drips of thawing snow from the face of the Appalachian range, with its great ear cocked southward for the muffled cries of returning geese. The march of Spring gathered momentum on the flood tide of rivers grown wild and drunk with rain, where hungry trout, stacked cheek by jowl in the current, struggled for their place at the long-awaited banquet of flies—an abundance nearly forgotten in the months of ice and sleep, sleep and ice.

By July the journey slowed considerably and seemed to stand still in thick forests, dark and heavy with the smell of rain. There, you and I hung our tarps and found a tree good for leaning paddles, while we fetched supper from the bottom of a canvas pack. We dared not speak, that afternoon, of the impossibly blue sky, or of how the fish had been so easily fooled, or that in all the days that had been spent in the woods for a hundred generations, no one could have seen a finer example of a bull moose than the one that surprised us at the end of the portage. If we spoke of these things, perhaps they would disappear, we worried. Perhaps the weather gods might realize that they had overlooked our daily dram of misery for days on end, and it would blow a gale all the way to Kittery. So we smiled without a word as the woods beyond our campfire faded to grays and blues, and we slept like kings and emperors beneath a royal canopy of stars.

Deep within us we kindled a tiny flame of hope that this would be the year that the feast of our freedom would roll on forever. The immortal green of each leaf along the lake offered no hint of the dying golds and reds of autumn hidden within. The sunlight that painted the skies and the distant mountains betrayed no inkling of the planets above, quietly marking their appointed rounds through the portals of time, space and season.

A Dream of Spring

We had no cause to think of the end of things. Ours was only to begin anew each day—to swim, ebullient and naked, beneath the waterfalls. Ours was only to lay basking in the patch of sun that found its way through the fir tops onto the wide, flat rocks below. We had forgotten each and everything, all and anything, else. We had forgotten all of it because there was no one in the forest to remind us, and the sunshine made a hash of our memory.

Such luck, it was! Who knew that the Conservateur des Forêts would sign the wrong form for our camping permit—the blue one labeled "jamais plus" (nevermore)—and thereby cede to us all of Quebec, in error? The general populace had no choice but to move away and take most of the mosquitoes with them.

The two of us were left to paddle and camp over all three hundred twenty million acres, forever! Well, not forever, technically. You calculated that if we kept our pace we would reach the last lake in Quebec at about the same time the sun burned out. The whole affair caused a huge ruckus in Ottawa, but forms are forms—and the ones signed in triplicate, addressed to Her Royal Highness the Queen, can't be fixed. It was all ours.

In Summer, we were no different than the deer, the otter and the bear, you and I. We shared their world and for a week

or two dared imagine
that we belonged
with them. After all,
did not the paddle
bend to our whim?
Did not our slender
canoe sweep beneath
us like a woman who
has danced with the
same man all her life
and is as easily led by
his thoughts as by his
hand? Masters of
forest and stream,
our serenade was the
timeless song of the
whippoorwill, and
the barred owl
invited us every day
at evening to discuss
with him the great
issues of the age.

In that magic
haze, in that place
where we hung a
rope over a deep hole
for swimming, where
all men are boys,
time did stand still
for us that day in
July. It came at that
same moment when
you and I decide, as
we do each year, that
there shall be a Fall.

Somewhere between the first cup of coffee and the last strip of bacon at breakfast, one day, we decide that there again must be taxes and traffic jams, mortarboards and mortgages, football and apple cider and pumpkins and shiny shoes on the feet of little schoolchildren. And so there are such things. Time marches on, they say, but Man is the grand marshall of his own parade through Time, and what if we forgot to call Time's tune? To what, then, would Time march?

I tell you, my friend, Pogo was right when he said, "I have met the enemy, and he is us!" If we had just kept our eyes open and our thoughts clear, if we had lived in that moment of joy and that moment alone, who can say that all of us—every last one of us—would not still be there beside a campfire, on a lake, beneath a July moon? No, you say? No? Ah, but so little faith in the magic of daydreams, there is. Who, after all, are you to say "no"—you who looked away, you who let Summer slip past us like a fickle schoolgirl? You've done it again, don't you see? She was too fast for you, and wiser than her years. You climbed the rock above the lake to pick a prize of blueberries for her, then lost yourself in the thicket of a long, sinking afternoon. By the time you finally stumbled out on the other shore, fat and blue-faced, she had stolen your clothes and left with September. And now where have they gotten you, all of your promises of eternal love beneath an Adirondack moon?

Gather our paddles and let us go home. Enough of this fog. The tide is away, and Fall is upon us, with Winter on her heels. Let us finally say it and confront the bitterness of saying so: She is gone, our lovely Summer. She is as gone as a first kiss and the girl who gave it, and there is no turning back to either of them. Fond remembrance will warm us awhile but leave us colder still for the remembering. Like aging champions, we trundle through November along the paths of June, as the lakes close over again for spite at our inattention.

A day of unexpected warmth in December will tempt our memories, and we will pause for a moment at the edge of a field. We will crane our necks for a breath of Summer that travels on the wind like a lover's letter, but it will not be her. Tomorrow will be colder still. Soon there will be snow, and we will come at last to admit defeat at the grave of February.

What's that, you say? Kindle hope, you say? Why should we? She is gone, I tell you, and there is nothing but January and despair and ice in our boots. We had her beauty and all of Canada, too, and we gave them both up for this wind and bitterness. Leave me then to my pipe and fire, and do not torment me to speak of those halcyon days of August and the smell of pine in the noon sun.

Look, you say? Out there, in the distance? Look at what? There is nothing here but duty, news, and news of duty. There is much work to do, and I shall not go looking with you. Not at all. We had our chance.

Look, look farther you say, again? What is it that you see? I tell you she is gone, and the one you claim to see is a poor pretender to the throne of my heart. Her name is Spring you

say, but I do not know her. I have eyes only for Summer— Summer who left me to weep for her golden hair and bronzed shoulders. Do not tempt me with talk of hope, and leave me to my grief.

Will you not desist? Alright, then, I shall look for what little good it will do us. But wait—what is it, there? Yes, I now see what you see. She is shy, distant, and pale—but how lovely! Spring, you say? I see her now, yes. Still months away, I watch as she slowly slips off a long white gown of snow and stands shivering in the flesh. Such full, firm breasts, and cheeks still flush from the cold. The gentle curve of her back meets her hips and forms the shape of a heart that would steal my own. She fixes my eyes like a talisman. I cannot look away. It is no use any longer to mourn. I am in love! I am in love, and her name is Spring! There shall never be another like her, and none so splendid or fine. We shall soon be wild and drunk with rain, she and I, on rivers of melting snow, in meadows where no man for a hundred generations has seen such sights as we shall find. Come with us, will you? We will not fail her, this time. To Canada! To Canada, boys! Spring is ours, and we are hers, and cruel December has lost its might.

While Ye May

Summer 1996

As I prepared for our voyage in the Adirondacks
this summer, I thought it behooved me to read
an excellent book about the life and letters of
one of the first white men to go venturing by canoe
without a professional guide in this wilderness of upstate
New York. The book is *Canoeing the Adirondacks with
Nessmuk; the Adirondack Letters of George Washington
Sears*, published by the Adirondack Museum at Blue
Mountain Lake. It is edited by Dan Brenan, with
revisions by Robert L. Lyon and Hallie E. Bond. The
book compiles the several letters written by Sears in the
1880's for *Forest & Stream* magazine, under the
Narragansett Indian pen-name "Nessmuk," about his
canoe-camping adventures in the Adirondacks.

Editor Dan Brenan credits Nessmuk for the
"democratization of wilderness travel" that has made
outdoor recreation the industry and passion of millions

that it is today. In Nessmuk's time, those who came to the Adirondacks for its storied trout-fishing and deer hunting generally were "sports." They would hire a guide to transport them from lake to lake in a distinctively-shaped rowing canoe known as the Adirondack guide boat. Nessmuk clearly admired and revered the guides for their skill and knowledge of the woods, but he sought more to emulate than be served by them. At 5-feet 3-inches tall and 110 pounds, however, he could, one supposes, only with great difficulty portage a guide boat that typically weighed 75 pounds or more. Seeking a more self-reliant experience, he commissioned the construction of short, lightweight boats that later became commonly referred to as "pack" canoes. One such boat, which he named the *Sairy Gamp*, measured just 9 feet and weighed 10-1/2 pounds. The published letters of his Adirondack trips "going through alone" in these small boats fanned the popularity of the design and, Brenan concludes, helped to usher in the "golden age" of American canoeing.

Despite his determined independence, love for the outdoors, and remarkably skilled woodcraft, Nessmuk's poor health, Brenan notes, was a recurrent nuisance that sometimes interfered with or interrupted his adventures. He was afflicted by malaria and the respiratory illnesses common to that era. In his last years, Nessmuk wrote the following in a letter to a friend, who had invited him on a trip to seek respite from his condition: "I seldom get beyond the front yard, and the gun is of no further use to me, while I have not put the old rod together in two years. Time and 'physical disability' will . . . beat every mother's son of us and I do not complain. Few men have had as much of life in the woods as I have, and memory at least can not be taken away from me while my senses hold good . . . Ah me! how vividly I recall the visit, all too short, that we had at the Moose River years ago. *Tempus fugit* [time flies]. Let him fly; let him flicker. I have been there, and done it; and if I were young again I would do it some more . . ."

In our age of vaccines, long life, and unprecedented wellness, it is easy for us who are the progeny of Nessmuk's self-reliant ideal to forget that life holds no guarantees, and that our own days of wilderness sojourning might not be long. I recall once telling an elderly woman about my idle dreams to someday cruise the world in a sailboat—a pursuit that Nessmuk had also enjoyed—but dismissing lightheartedly the notion that work and family ties would soon, if ever, permit such a trip. She paused to answer, and, with an abrupt seriousness and unsolicited concern for my plans, flatly said . . . "go now." It was clear to me from the depth of her glance, seemingly across the span of a lifetime, that she offered knowledge distilled from experience. *Tempus fugit.* It is said that no one on his death bed ever wished for more time at the office. Our "Adirondack days," wherever spent among friends and family, are the ones that we, like Nessmuk, will treasure most in the end.

The Living Wilderness

Winter 1998

My grandfather George Washington LaCroix was raised on a farm near Pulaski, Tennessee. I have only a fleeting memory of him, when I was two, as the old man in the bed on the second floor of my grandmother's house in Baltimore, just before he died. His younger brothers Jefferson Davis ("Jeff") and Monroe ("Monnie") had stayed and made a living through the Great Depression in the gentle hills where "George W" was born.

Right after Christmas, in 1972, I left Baltimore and headed south for a first visit with my grandfather's side of the family. In my mother's judgment I was getting to an age, at 14, that demanded more freedom of movement than our small apartment in the suburbs could furnish. I was about to encounter, and be distinctly changed by, a world vastly different from the one that I knew.

The differences in that new world were apparent to my every sense from the first step I took inside Uncle Jeff's and Aunt Viola's tin-roof farmhouse, tucked back in Puryear Hollow. Theirs was a life lived very close to the land. The woodstove in the main bedroom provided the only (and ample) heat in winter. The fields behind the house produced tobacco and cattle for the auction houses, hay for the animals in winter, and vegetables of every variety for the table.

For more than a century, the LaCroix family had trapped the creeks and streams of this area for mink and muskrat and hunted the hills all about for squirrel, rabbit, and deer. Even among a rural community accustomed to such living, Jeff and Viola were widely noted for having raised their two, giant sons largely on a diet of wild game.

There was a rugged honesty and toughness to this way of life that intrigued me. Although I was an athlete of average ability, the lifestyle I encountered among my grandfather's family demanded a different sort of grit. They had a mental and physical toughness forged by the elements and measured in terms more subtle than time, speed, and points scored.

The days after Christmas are the last of the deer-hunting season in Tennessee and most everywhere else. I was outfitted with a brand-new pair of leather, Herman Survivor boots and a goose-down coat purchased for me by a neighbor who knew I had little of what I would need for a winter hunting-trip. In my own mind I was every inch of Davy Crockett, but that image quickly faded.

The LaCroix men weren't equipped the way I was or the way I expected them to be, nor did it seem to matter much. They had an eye for useful things, but not much use for luxury. While in the woods one day I was dressed to the nines and freezing my tail off, bouncing from one foot to the other to keep warm despite the goose down, leather gloves, and 40-below-zero boots. At the same time my Uncle Monnie, a man then in his sixties, kept vigil in a light, cloth jacket, holding a cold rifle-stock in his thick, bare hands without complaint. How, in such circumstances, do you say to a man fifty years your senior that you are freezing and need to head in? Pride goeth, and I decided to follow. Monnie didn't mind, of course, but his seeming indifference to the elements left an impression on me.

I eagerly returned to Tennessee for the next two summers. In that time I learned a little more about life on the land and took my post as Defender of the Bean Fields against the willful incursions of cottontail rabbits. I would watch as Uncle Jeff, slowed only by the arthritis in his fingers, expertly dressed the fish and game that the earth yielded to us, to be breaded, pan-fried and served for supper. The leftovers were saved, reheated and served again at the next meal, until all was gone.

"Wilderness adventures" in this world were not planned—they simply occurred. Jeff's son Charles and I once

took off for someplace on the Little Tennessee River without much more than a boat and a bottle of peach soda between us. Neither he nor I can recall the spot, but I'll never forget the trip. When night fell, we found a high, rock ledge overlooking the river and laid our bedrolls on the open ground. Gazing up in the pitch black at the dazzling array of stars, we wondered out loud about Chariots of the Gods, life, and the origin of things.

During an entirely different type of adventure, I got to know a tomboy who lived at the next farm up the road. Until then I had never even kissed a girl, but by the end of that first summer I was as certain as only a 15-year old boy can be that I would never love another. Now married and a mother of two, she never knew that I stayed up all night before my flight home, scrawling elaborate plans at the kitchen table for an escape into the woods. There, in the name of true love, I intended to seek sanctuary from the cruel imperatives of growing up. It was only the certain knowledge that my sanity would forevermore be in doubt that persuaded me otherwise. Despite these reservations, though, I never paused to wonder whether the forest would provide for my needs.

Impossibly, it has been more than twenty-six years since that first Tennessee holiday. What you now hold in your hands is grown from the seeds of that experience. I often wonder whether we in this country are still planting such seeds—or enough of them.

Last summer, my eight-year old son and I chanced to share a group campsite for one night with a patrol of boy scouts who, like us, were on a canoe trip through the Adirondacks. Notable in their routine was the complete absence of a campfire. Propane stoves and lanterns were humming everywhere, but not one stick of wood was kindled for cooking or camaraderie. Most of their food was reconstituted from plastic bags, all without preparation or cooking over an open flame. They did not occupy their time fishing for dinner, nor with pioneering. There was not an axe, a saw, a filet knife, or a Dutch oven to be found among them. They were *at* the woods but not *in* the woods.

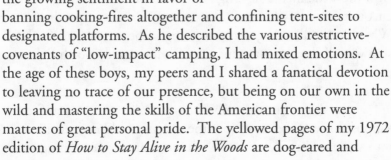

A friend whose son is in the scouts explained to me that rustic camping has fallen out of favor with some wilderness advocates. He cited the growing sentiment in favor of banning cooking-fires altogether and confining tent-sites to designated platforms. As he described the various restrictive-covenants of "low-impact" camping, I had mixed emotions. At the age of these boys, my peers and I shared a fanatical devotion to leaving no trace of our presence, but being on our own in the wild and mastering the skills of the American frontier were matters of great personal pride. The yellowed pages of my 1972 edition of *How to Stay Alive in the Woods* are dog-eared and underlined. It occurred to me that, with a very different sense of themselves as aliens unwelcome to touch or tarry in this world, the "impact" of this new type of wilderness experience would be low, indeed—on the boys who were having it. The magic of canoe-tripping, after all, lies in the re-creation of a way of life connected to the land, not the ability merely to "withstand" the elements through a brief triumph of portable technology.

I join with those who seek to reduce man's impact where the very notion of "wilderness" is threatened by it. There surely are wild places we have loved too much; but I wonder if the problem is so widespread as we may suppose. Every year I paddle and camp extensively in varied parts of this country, and it is astounding in this age how often I am utterly alone. My abiding concern is less for canoeists' impact on the wilderness than that there are not enough children furloughed on a more regular basis from the malls, arcades, and soccer fields to interact with—and be impacted by—the very places which we must look to them to preserve.

Do you remember the first time you saw the Great Smoky Mountains? Did you look out over the purple haze and imagine the world as it was before the first axe fell on these shores? Did you plan, as I did, to follow a tumbling, crystal stream to that place where the "big ones" were hiding? Did you dream of a hidden falls, the perfect cast, the impossible trout? If so, ask yourself: Do we allow such places to infect our children with the same incurable longing, or will brief, technological encounters with wild places leave no trace on their psyches? When duty calls this generation to fight the next wave of urban sprawl, will they have a romance with the woods worth fighting for?

Looking into the embers of our Adirondack campfire, I supposed it was useless to join the chorus of old codgers pining for the way things "used to be." Time marches on. Things change. Just then, my son Kip came into camp. By the firelight I saw that he had the face of a coal miner, and what clothes remained attached to his body were covered in mud. He would need a long swim in the morning, but he was asleep before his head hit the blanket. I decided that if what sticks to him in these woods never washes off entirely, that will be just fine with me.

Traveling Light

Spring 1999

In my last year of law school, at the start of a final exam in one particularly difficult course, several dozen of my classmates and I were spaced evenly apart in the auditorium, each with nothing upon his desk but a pen and a blank exam booklet. This arrangement was designed to prevent cheating. The distance between students made it impossible for anyone to see what anyone else was writing in his exam book, and any extraneous material on one's desk would be easily spotted.

Before the start of the exam, I saw the professor approach one young man and ask to see a small card on his desk. It turned out to be a holy card. These are small cards illustrated with a scene from the Gospel and imprinted with a prayer. They are used by many Catholics as an aid to faith in times of need or special devotion. This being a Jesuit school, the professor was only too pleased to allow the card to remain.

As I said, it was a difficult course. Sometime during the test, I noticed the young man in question draw a card from his pocket. Whether it was the same card the professor had examined earlier I cannot tell you and am only too happy not to know; but the furtive manner in which it was retrieved and read suggested to me that the young man's purpose was something other than prayer. That image has endured in my memory because it was so starkly unexpected. He was one of the brighter students in the class.

In the years since law school I have preferred to give my classmate the benefit of the doubt. But whatever idealism I took with me on graduation day has been sorely tested in the ensuing fifteen years of trial practice and daily life. I have seen judges, lawyers, paupers and princes cheat with gusto and devotion. None of these sins was committed for a loaf of bread or medicine for a sick child. With few exceptions, they were lies told out of a desire for material gain or the fear of material loss—told by people who, like the young law student, were well able to achieve their desires and assuage their fears through honorable means.

It is symptomatic of our human nature, in general, and our American culture, in particular, that we seek to surround ourselves with a superabundance of material comforts. I need hardly bother to make this point heard above the deafening roar of Madison Avenue which shouts it every day. There are creams that make us look young and cars that make us look rich. There are houses that make us feel powerful and gadgets that make us feel smart. There are baubles and trifles and curios without number to clutter our cabinets and speak of our good taste, and there are malls without end to store and sell them. There are clubs and societies and schools and neighborhoods that make us feel well-connected or well-bred. And then there are the clothes and ornaments we find pleasing because they reassure us (and remind others) that we are the kind of people who would own

the cars, go to the schools, belong to the clubs, and live in such neighborhoods as we do. In this way are our days enslaved—not in a struggle against want but in a pledge of fealty to the things of this world. What a fool's lot this is.

Lest my purpose be misunderstood, let me hasten to confess my full-paid, charter membership in this fraternity of fools. It is a decided minority in this country whose homes are not a palace, whose dinner tables are not a banquet, and whose furnishings are not a royal dowry in the currency of the wider world. If we are to hear the voice of Mr. Lincoln's "better angels," we must step away from the crowd. When we do, we will often find we have wandered into the wilderness.

My first encounter with the transforming power of wilderness happened to occur in a sailboat. I was with my

73

brother on the South River of Chesapeake Bay in a Rhodes 19 that he had rented by the hour. The boat had no motor, but I recall looking over the bow at the unbroken horizon and realizing that it was within our power, at that moment, to sail as long and far as the water and wind would bear us. What an epiphany that was to me, and how well it illustrates what I have recognized elsewhere in life's wiser moments. It is the promise of that which is sustainable, incorruptible, unfailing and unfettered which marks the eternal.

In the simple form of the canoe we find not only a means of travel and amusement but an opportunity to sever ties to a needlessly complex world. Less truly is more. Furnished in nothing more than what a common man's wages might buy, I have never known an hour of want in the woods. The excesses of domestic life may accumulate unnoticed in our closets, but in the middle of a day's fourth portage, any undue luxury in our packs will surely declare itself.

It is not to be all sackcloth and ashes, this life. There is a time to break out the best wine, strike up the band, and let the good times roll. In the woods it has pleased me to fete friends and family with what luxuries I could conceive and the frame of a canoe could carry. Traveling alone, though, we have time and need for introspection. On a solo voyage a man has no one to please but himself, and his self-regard appreciates no flattery. It is fitting to travel light when traveling alone and to take only that which is needed or perhaps a little less—the better to discern our wants from our needs and steer a straighter course between the two.

I have lately been amused by an advertisement for a financial service of some sort appearing in *The Wall Street Journal*. The caption, paraphrasing Henry David Thoreau's command, tells the reader to go confidently in the direction of his dreams. The man in the photograph is a study in the nonchalance of wealth, and he appears to be going confidently in the direction of a rather large, beachfront estate in the Hamptons. I wonder what the author of *The Maine Woods* would say to that. It will take a lot more than confidence to make headway in the direction of that particular dream. Yet this is the siren song of popular culture—mainstream culture, mind you—and every day another man drives his ship upon the rocks in pursuit of it. As often as you and I sleep beneath the trees, kindle a campfire for our comfort, and fish for our dinner, we will hear a different song.

In this season of penance, therefore, let me waste no time to make my pledge: I aspire to die a man of modest means in a modest house, having frittered away my chance for fame and fortune in the pursuit of quiet lakes, distant shores, and deep woods. I aspire to know my family better than my friends and my friends better than my clients. I aspire to make something of my life, not something of myself. I aspire to be driving the same old Jeep long after the neighbors start whispering.

As well as I know the distance between my reach and my grasp, I know I will falter in these ambitions. It is no modest house I live in now, and no modest man who lives there. But if God should grant that you outlive me, heaven help me if when you come to pay your last respects you find only men and women of "high esteem" in attendance. Pray for me if there is not one there who can say that I gave him a dollar when he didn't really need it and my coat when he did. When the papers write that they found Hurley's last camp, let it be said that there was no more in his pack than was rightly needed for a good night's shelter, a warm fire, and a decent meal. Let it be said of me and of all of us that we traveled light through this world, ever mindful of the world to come.

Memories of Maine

Fall 1996

In the spring of 1977, I sat by the window of my dormitory room at Western Maryland College, unable to sleep one night at 3:00 a.m. As I looked down on the little town of Westminster, at the foot of the Catoctin Mountains, my thoughts were not of school or studies but of the plans for the coming summer, and where I would be. A well-worn James Taylor LP crackled wistfully in the background—the preferred mood-maker of my generation for just such late-night ruminations.

I don't recall today exactly what frame of reference I had for the State of Maine at the age of 19, having never traveled there before nor being able to name a solitary person who lived there, save someone named L. L. Bean. Perhaps I was inspired by the vintage photographs of my 1940's-era fishing encyclopedia, showing men in buffalo-plaid shirts and fedoras hoisting the coveted smallmouth bass—the harder caught, better

tasting, and scrappier fighter of the species—from clear, granite lakes amid the wilderness.

Perhaps it was an image I had conjured up from a decade of Bean catalogs of this hardy, fir-crested territory, populated by men who supped clam chowder and black coffee and lived the kind of authentic sporting experience that most suburban kids could only read about in the pages of *Field & Stream*.

Whatever my expectations were, by the morning I was busy calling and writing a dozen or more summer camps seeking employment as a counselor. One that replied and offered me a position overseeing a cabin full of junior campers was the venerable Kennebec boys' camp of the Belgrade Lakes region.

Within a scant few days of my late-night insomnia, my plans for a summer in Maine were well in hand. Certainly it was not the first nor hardly the last of many wild hares I would conceive from thin air, unaided by the advice or experience of others. But if it was tradition, beauty, and a flavor of old Maine summers I sought, I would find it here in spades.

I arrived at the Kennebec Camps with a battalion of other counselors and staff in early June to begin the advance preparations for the season. Piles of equipment and gear were pulled out of cabins and sheds where they had been secured against the ravages of the Maine winter. The beachfront was readied for the campers at Salmon Pond, whose waters were so frigid that full wetsuits were required for the task of re-floating and securing the swim docks. Yard after yard of tape was carefully tapped into place on the only real-clay tennis courts I had ever seen. Log cabins and pine-wood mess halls were swept and cleaned. Dozens of canoes were gently set in place by the pond amid rows of paddles.

Salmon Pond, with its crystalline water and fir trees pointing like steeples to the sky around its shores, was a glorious sight to a boy from Baltimore. To this day it embodies my sense of the classic Maine lake country. It is no wilderness, to be sure, but as is often the feel one gets elsewhere in Maine, the character and simplicity of its few cottages lend a certain charm all their own.

It was apparent to me, from faded photographs lining the cabin walls, that the Kennebec Camps had been operating in much the same fashion for decades before I arrived. On each opening weekend old campers would return to their alma mater for a reunion, and in this particular year they came back in droves—platoons of old men with widening girths and bald heads made young again in Indian head-dresses and face paint, racing each other in war canoes down the pond to settle old scores. The traditions of this grand old place were everywhere in evidence.

In sturdy wood-canvas canoes that had obviously delivered years of good service, with many more to come, we ferried young campers that summer to the woods around Salmon Pond to spend nights in tents and sleeping bags. The water was so clean we dipped it in buckets from the lake for drinking and dove for mussels from the sandy bottom.

The pond was deeper at the middle than I was ever able to fathom. Serious fishermen would occasionally glide by, and I once saw what appeared to be a near-record smallmouth that ambushed an angler from a granite ledge near our camp. I would later recall with incredulity that, in the entire summer I spent in this paradise in 1977, I never wet a line. My one encounter with a smallmouth bass was eye to eye, underwater, in the shade beneath the dock. While swimming there I stopped to notice a lunker finning his way idly by, with almost no concern for my presence. Perhaps the fish understood that I was of an age where matters of fishing and outdoor life had taken a back seat to romance. In any event, the bass population of Salmon Pond was no match for a young girl I had met at a church in Augusta, and to whom I beat a path whenever furloughed for an afternoon from my duties at camp.

One day this young lady and I traveled north to Bar Harbor to see the sights from atop the seaside mountains of that glorious venue. There is no place in America quite like it. On our way home, we encountered another enchanted place that now remains only in the Brigadoon mists of my distant memory and has never fully re-emerged. We stopped at a summer theater attended by, excepting ourselves, a rather well-to-do crowd. I recall neither its name nor its location within three hundred miles, but it was a large, white clapboard meeting house, theater, or auditorium of some kind set amid rows of old trees and

pathways that led
through beautiful
gardens and lawns.
Perhaps it was
somewhere near the
French-speaking
region of Maine, or
perhaps I am
mistaken. I wish I
could find it again,
but no one to whom I
have spoken about my
experience knows of
such a place. We
spent an evening,
there, enjoying a live
performance of Joseph
Stein's *Fiddler on the
Roof.* Many are
familiar with this story
of the character Tevye's
lament. Amid my
fading memories of
this place, that day,
and the girl I came
with, the refrain of the
booming ode to
"tradition" in this
musical remains clear.
It was a stirring
tribute, in this place so
steeped in the
traditions of summer,
to a value that I did
not fully appreciate at
the time.

The summer passed too quickly, and I soon found myself headed back to the hills of Western Maryland. Correspondence with the young lady from Augusta fell to a trickle, then stopped altogether, and later college summers were spent on other far-flung (though less enchanting) adventures. Still, the seeds of my own traditions had been sown, and fourteen years later I would return with my wife and infant son to a cottage from that earlier summer—more of a mind, at the age of 33, to give the bass their due. I was not disappointed by the fish or the place, and I knew I would return again and again.

The Allagash voyage reported in this issue is a reprise of these earlier pilgrimages to Maine, now nearly twenty years after my first encounter with its granite lakes. Its magnificence is undiminished. As I sat atop the thundering Allagash Falls this summer, I marveled at the power of a tradition—conceived on a sleepless night two decades earlier and nurtured on the milk of memory—to draw me back to these hallowed woods.

The Adventurous Life

Winter 1996

In a hotel restaurant in downtown Houston, in 1988, I sat uneasily at the table with two attorneys from one of the nation's largest companies. Having just recently taken a leap of faith in opening my own law office after four years of employment with a firm, I faced the unfamiliar task of explaining why a 30-year old upstart—with a one-room office and a computer—was a good choice to handle litigation for a company that typically hires law firms with hundreds of employees.

The senior lawyer inquired as to the number of paralegals on my staff. I answered that there were none. Silence followed. I recovered with an anxious explanation of the wondrous capabilities of my new 8-megahertz PC and an astonishing program called WordPerfect. The other lawyer, who was a young friend of mine, volunteered some mitigators to my lack of staff. At length, though, the older lawyer eased back in his

chair and asked me why I had done it— why I had left the security of a respected law firm and a steady paycheck to hit the street without a single case or client to my credit. My rather cavalier and hastily-conceived answer to this man, who I would guess was some twenty years my elder, was that I did not want to spend my old age regretting that I had never tried. Again, silence. I'm sure at that point I must have begun looking among the dinner mints for a new career, but then I heard the man say that he often wished he'd done the same at my age. It was not the most digestible lunch I can recall, but I got the business, and my practice grew.

In the years that followed, relatives would visit and ask how business was going and whether I'd "made

it" yet. When I would explain that there was no "it" to make—
that success or failure in any professional practice was always
looming in the next case—they clearly were unsatisfied. Their
unease on the subject called to mind a crowd watching a Hail
Mary pass by an untested quarterback. Hope and regret, glory
and condemnation, are suspended together with the ball. But in
life and business, the ball never really comes all the way back
down, and the pass is not completed until the end of the game.

Not too long after that lunch I decided to show my
gratitude to Anna, the young lawyer who had spoken for me, by
torturing her and her fiancée on a weekend cruise. We were
returning a sailboat from Port O'Connor to Houston.
Landlubbers both, they had signed on for the voyage in the
expectation that we would spend our time gliding up the Texas
coast, waving ashore under puffy, white clouds and blue skies.
But as many who have traveled with me can attest, the reality of
life's adventures sometimes falls short, sometimes far exceeds, but
is certainly always different from what we dream in sheltered
evenings by the fireside. We soon found ourselves close hauled
and punching through long swells on a course headed offshore
in the blackening night. When it was Anna's watch, she crawled
out of the forward berth, where she'd no doubt taken a good
head-pounding for the past four hours, and took a grip on the
tiller. On the horizon, a light rose dimly out of the darkness.
Those on shore might have remarked at what a pretty sight it
was, but to Anna, in the fearsome, unforgiving darkness of a
night at sea, it was a "blood red moon."

Let purveyors of ocean-going adventure say what they
will: Riding a breakable, sinkable, fiberglass shell over fifteen
fathoms of roiling, blue-green mystery, far from shore, is a
marked risk. As I looked down from the cockpit that night at
the sea whooshing past, just inches below the rail, I found no
words for Anna to ameliorate the essential danger and
uncertainty of our position. This was no thrill ride at an

amusement park. That really was Davy Jones' locker below us, and yes, all that came between us and the briny deep were our nerve and a bit of plastic. Yet on my wall now hangs a painting given to me in fond memory of that voyage. And who among us does not harbor a romantic notion of someday sailing to tropic seas in command of a tiny vessel?

The sense of those nights at sea came rushing back to me as we ventured steadily farther into the roadless wilderness of Northern Minnesota, last summer. We were placing ourselves in a circumstance of dependency on the elements and, with each paddle stroke toward the north, becoming a little less able to make radical or swift alterations in that dependency for whatever reason that might have arisen. The vapor-thin, Kevlar hull of our rented canoe resounded with a sickening "crack!" over rocks in the shallow flows. Mentally, we ran through the permutations of various disasters: finding ourselves with an irreparable canoe on some forgotten beaver-flow a hundred miles from the nearest road; losing our provisions to bears; a broken leg or injured back half-way into the voyage; a sudden attack of appendicitis and a race against time to reach help.

On the third day of our Minnesota trip, after gorging ourselves on blueberries at the end of Sunday Lake, we set happily about a course on the Beartrap River that we expected would take us eventually north into Iron Lake. It was getting toward mid-afternoon on a cloudy, gray day. Slowly, the channel in the river grew narrow among the lily pads and grass, and then narrower still. Soon, we were straining to keep the canoe moving forward through barely visible water overgrown with thick vegetation. After it seemed clear that we had lost any discernible channel, we stopped. We looked at the map, then at the scene around us, then at the map. We stood up in the boat. No answers. The map depicted a clearly discernible ribbon of blue where the river was supposed to be—and no doubt was in colder months. But we were in the middle of a seamless marsh

appearing to stretch for miles in every direction. If we chose to go on a given course to look for the channel and guessed wrong, it could be hours and near dark before we realized our error.

Although we weren't stumped for long, had one of us not noticed some unusual topography on the map near the northward bend in the river and matched that to a bluff we could see in the distance, we might have been lost quite a while longer. But in the moments we were stopped, there, the sense of risk was palpable. There were no guarantees and no easy answers. No cheery words could remit the need to regain our course, nor soften the hazards of failing to do so.

In the woods as in life, it is instructive at times simply to stop and absorb the profound, unblinking reality of the world around us. There in the silence is a challenge that goads us to risk foot-less paths. "Do what you will," it says. "Find your way or not," it says. "I will be here as a witness to the ages; mute, pitiless, and immovable." No man can foresee what that challenge portends for him, but in what we cannot foresee yet dare to discover lies the heart of adventure. And whether we succeed or fail in our endeavors, we shall always be glad to say that we attempted the journey.

The Simple Life

Spring 1997

At a campsite along the route of the Adirondack Canoe Classic, a few years ago, I overheard a conversation between two of the participants in that three-day, ninety-mile marathon. One was an older gentleman, a veteran of many years in the race. His movements were deliberate and unhurried whether he was paddling or progressing through the familiar rituals of an evening in camp. That night his rumpled, old canvas tent was set up on the banks of Forked Lake. Everything in his outfit appeared well-worn, and I dare say he had not purchased a new item of gear in many years. As the two talked, the older man inquired about the younger fellow's career and his busy life back in the big city. The young man gave an accounting of how life had treated him since the previous year's race. As he did so he mentioned with a sigh that there were of course a good many items of gear and other things he'd like to acquire but for which there never seemed to be enough money or

time. The older man was unmoved. Then he replied to his young friend with some advice that struck me as rather profound: "It's not how much money you have," he said, "but what you spend it on." Clearly the older gentleman had spent his money sparingly and wisely over the years on an outfit that continued to serve him well at little or no additional expense.

As I considered this man's advice, I began to realize how applicable it was across a wide set of circumstances. My wife and I married two weeks after graduating from college and resolved to put ourselves through law school together without financial assistance from our families. In those years the only money we made was through student work-study programs and summer clerkships, all of which added up to less than the federal poverty-line in our most prosperous year. I have a sense of the five loaves and two fishes now when I look back at our tax returns for those years and wonder how we ever made it, but at the time we felt solidly planted in the middle class. Our lives were less cluttered with things, our diversions were simpler, our commitments were fewer, and our time was our own. As the years went by we saw more prosperity, but we were no happier because of it.

When we finally entered private practice, we would occasionally rub elbows with some "high rollers" in the business and legal community. As a rule they lived in huge, ludicrously expensive homes, and to me their private lives seemed to be guided by the most superfluous and trivial concerns. This predictably yielded for them more unhappiness in the form of broken hearts, drug and alcohol abuse, and depression than was usually visited upon serfs like us in our tiny apartments on tiny budgets. All of this was cause for frequent introspection on my part about the real meaning of the "American Dream" and my place within it. That introspection has yielded no easy answers but rather a number of observations.

There is a tendency toward voracious consumption in our culture that is pervasive. The American dream in the minds of millions has come to mean a continually upward spiral of material largesse: a bigger paycheck, a bigger house on a larger lot in a better neighborhood, more clothes, more expensive vacations, and generally greater self-indulgence than our parents' generation could conceive. A love of spending for its own sake and a steady expansion in the inventory of our wardrobes, furnishings, and accessories are articles of faith in the new American mall-culture. It has been reported that the average new home built today is some 40 percent larger than the average new home built in the 1950's, leaving one to wonder how Mom and Dad ever managed to raise a family for all those years in that little ranch house. Real estate agents now refer to a home that an upper middle-class family of the previous generation might have worked their entire lives to afford as a "good starter." Well, who moved the finish line?

It is not that our parents lived deprived lives; it is rather that our perspective has changed. The bar for an acceptable minimum lifestyle has been raised almost imperceptibly over the years by the steady march of Madison Avenue to the point where, now, life without two cars, two televisions, a microwave, videos, cable TV, frequent dinners out, seventy-five-dollar leather sneakers, health clubs, and a phalanx of scheduled activities for even the youngest of children is considered a hardship. Yet many of us who tend to accept this mentality as part of mainstream American culture—myself included—fail to appreciate the clutter and complexity, not to mention the expense, it contributes to our lives. Not surprisingly, frustration is rising over a sense of declining quality of life amid nostalgia for the less frenetic pace of earlier times. Standing in stark contrast to these phenomena are people like that Adirondack canoeist, with a rumpled tent, an old boat, a well-dented stew pot, and other coddled items of equipment acquired through the years, who remind us that living well is more about making good choices than making a fortune.

The canoeist's advice was called to mind again this winter as I accompanied Virginian Fred Ostrander down the Nottoway River. Fred made the trip in the Old Town Otca canoe that he and his father had bought new in 1939 for $210. My first thought upon hearing the price was how very cheap it was compared to the cost of such boats today. My second thought was that if the entire American public followed Fred's shopping regimen, there would be no economy left. As I considered it further, however, I realized that $210 was a tidy sum in the dark days of 1939. Yet, the money Fred and his father had invested in what may have seemed to some at the time a pricey extravagance had been money well spent.

I suppose that there is the slightest whiff of elitism in this whole business of canoeing in general and even more so in the rarefied world of traditional canoes. They are not inexpensive craft, but as with any classic, when the immediate cost is amortized across the timelessness of their appeal, they become almost inexpensive by comparison. Which of your present possessions can you say you will have thirty or fifty years from now and be truly enriched for the money you spent to acquire it?

What draws us to voyaging by canoe is a simple elegance that has little to do in the long run with money or privilege. Once you have the boat and a paddle to make her go, the equation is fairly complete. There is more room for expense in the gear you take with you, but even this has its limit. Eventually you find that your needs are well met and that what remains is simply to go. If you set your sights on the essentials of the voyage and invest in equipment built to last, the return is exponential. Money could never purchase the glory of the sunrise over a remote, northern lake accessible only by canoe, or the thrill of coming face to face with a moose whose ancestors fed and clothed the earliest humans on the continent; yet for the small cost of pack, paddle and craft it is available to anyone who has the wisdom to gauge its real value.

Original
Wilderness
Illustrations

1995 ~ 2003

Self-portrait of the author, shaving aboard the S/V Whisper in Key Largo.

Long Lake Camp, Adirondacks

Coming ashore on the Suwannee

Caroline fishing for leaves in the Tyger.

Making Time to the Portage

Fooled Again.

Hurry Supper

A Lift-over on the James

Boundary Waters Lily Pads

Caroline at Cabbage Key

The Trooper

Caroline Wading in Churn Creek

Atop Mount Fredericka

King of Maine

The Kindness of Strangers

Fall 1996

On our first trip into Boston's airport, Julie was three-months pregnant with our daughter Caroline. Together we were moving our one-year old son and a mountain of luggage through cramped hallways, up and down escalators, and on crowded shuttle buses. We had brought everything we could think of and then some for a two-week vacation at a tiny cabin on a lake in Maine.

I remember this trip not because the bass in the lake were the most gullible I have encountered, before or since. The picture of that trip in my mind is of a dark, early morning when I sat up beside the wood stove, while Julie and our infant son slept in the other room. Worried as I often was about cases and clients and employees back at our law practice in Houston, I could not sleep. A Federal Express package of papers to review and sign had arrived the day before. Another would go

out that day. It was June 1991, and we had never been away from anything or anywhere for two weeks. While sitting in the dim, electric light of the cabin and jotting down "what if" scenarios on a scrap of paper, I conceived the idea that led, six months later, to the sale of our law practice, the move to North Carolina, a brief fling as a charterboat captain, and, in the fall of 1995, the first issue of this journal. There are three places where my life has made a dramatic, new beginning: One is the maternity ward at Johns Hopkins Hospital, circa 1958; one is the Sunshine Café in College Park, Maryland, where I proposed to my wife; and one is this cabin in Maine.

The driver who would bring the overnight packages to us and pick up new ones was intrigued to be making deliveries to the banks of Knickerbocker Lake. He had a genuine concern for our affairs that was almost quaint. If he didn't thoroughly enjoy his own job and wasn't sincerely interested in making sure I could do mine, he was doing an awfully good job of faking it. Not so for some of the other New Englanders we met on that trip.

Passengers and employees in the Boston airport at our coming and going could not have better epitomized a Southerner's stereotype of "Damn Yankees." There was pushing and shoving and utter lack of pity for a young mother with a baby and her clearly inept husband, trying to wend their way through the maze of concourses, gates, and lines. When at one point it became apparent that we had been deposited at the wrong end of the terminal and might miss our flight, the faces of those best able to help us could not have been more vacant of concern.

Not usually one to hold a grudge, I have made special exception for the Amtrak employees at Chicago's Union Station (another grim tale) and the folks Julie and I met on that trip in the Boston airport. And so it was with a sense of dread that I learned, on a return flight from Bangor this past summer, that I would be taking an unexpected detour through Beantown.

I suppose there are more serious things that the ground crew in Bangor could have forgotten to do than close the door to the airplane before we took off, but that was reason enough for the pilot to return to the airport. Back in Bangor, I was told that all of the available planes with fully closing doors were headed to Boston, where apparently they still have my name and photo on file under the words, "Do not help this man under any circumstance." I hopped aboard, made sure I heard the door slam shut, and hoped for the best.

It was par for the course that I would be the only one of twenty re-routed passengers to be given a voucher for a room that night in Boston at the "Parkway Plaza" hotel instead of the Ramada. I even shrugged it off when the Ramada shuttle bus promptly whisked all of the other passengers off to warm beds when we arrived at the airport at 1:00 a.m. A dark sense of destiny really didn't overcome me until I learned, at 2:00 a.m., that there *is no* Parkway Plaza hotel in Boston. There is a

Parkway Plaza hotel somewhere in Wyoming—and a lovely place it is, no doubt—but the name is spelled differently. Spelling is unimportant to airline clerks but a matter of national security to hotel managers.

The night manager of the "Park Plaza" hotel, a $200-per-night affair in downtown Boston, made it clear when I called from the airport that they would not accept vouchers for similarly named establishments located in Casper, Wyoming. But when I showed up anyway at 3:00 a.m. in his gleaming lobby, strapped to a muddy Duluth pack and dressed in the same clothes I had worn for the past three days on the St. Croix River, a sense of imminent danger must have overtaken him. I was given a free room with breakfast service, and I took full advantage of both.

Feeling as rested as circumstances would allow, the next morning, I did my best to look inconspicuous as I portaged past the concierge to a taxi at the curb. Back at the airport, fatigue finally got the best of me.

After returning one of those rented push-carts to its carousel, I was too busy digging for my 25-cent refund to notice that my camera case, containing $2,000 worth of equipment and all of the photographs you see in this issue, was still in the cart. I walked inside the terminal to a magazine stand to wait for my flight, not questioning why my hands were suddenly free to thumb through Claudia Schiffer's latest swimsuit pictorial.

You would have greater need for imagination in reading about the St. Croix River, in this issue, were it not for the kindness of a stranger at the airport in Boston—a resident of that fine city, no less. Having watched me leave the case in the cart, he had been looking for me for more than a few minutes when he walked up with my case in hand. Before the sudden rush that comes with disaster-nearly-missed would let me say more than

"thank you," the man nodded with a smile, and was gone. Never again will I paint all Bostonians with the same brush.

There is a lot of time for thinking on airplanes. On this recent trip from Boston I wondered why some of us hail the fellow-well-met in the wild, yet scarcely acknowledge those we meet on elevators, at intersections, and in airports. In gathering material for this journal I travel widely through the woods every year, often alone, in places I have never been before, and usually where I do not know a soul. The question I often get from friends and family is, "Aren't you afraid out there, where you don't know who might come along?" The answer is no. I can honestly say that I am more relaxed and unafraid for my safety in the woods than on any city street. The people I have met canoeing over the last thirty years have a lot more in common with that helpful fellow in the Boston airport than with whatever ghoulish characters might live in your imagination. Perhaps one reason for this is that, in the woods, I am a less ghoulish fellow, myself.

From the very first, people have regularly come along to lighten my load. The bundle of dry firewood handed to me one cold, wet night on the Allagash; packs carried three miles across a portage in the Adirondacks by two men I'd never met; room made for me in someone else's camp when it was too late to find my own—these are but a few of many examples that come to mind. For my part, I have tried to show others in the woods a measure of that kindness. Ah, but how quickly the spell fades when we return to the "civilized" world, as one sad example in my own life too clearly shows.

Having been informed that I am the last man in America whose wife prepares a hot meal every evening, I come when dinner is called and remain until the cook is finished. Ringing telephones are never answered during this ritual, but a knock at the door one night could not be ignored. When I turned on the porch light and opened the door, there in the darkness stood a man my age. Immediately, I realized he was selling something, and my defenses went up. From his pack he pulled several drawings, each carefully rendered with talent far beyond my own, and each selling for less than I would have accepted for poorer work. Awkwardly, and sensing he would be granted little time, he held a few examples out to their best advantage in the dim light. I complimented his work, but, eager to return to dinner, said I was "not interested" and bid him good night.

Sitting down, I looked across the table at the contented faces of my children. As I ruminated on the man's age and how badly I would have to need the money before I went door to door selling ten-dollar drawings, I realized there might be two similar faces looking across that man's table at an empty chair. I had turned away someone in need who had asked of me only a small measure of value for something of greater value in return. Had he wandered into my camp instead of my front yard, I would have known him as a friend. What is it in the city that closes men's hearts, or in the wilderness that opens them?

Returning to the door, I saw no one on our street. It hadn't been long. Perhaps a kinder neighbor had taken him in.

Or perhaps he had come only to bring this message to me, and to you: There are no strangers in this world. If "there but for the grace of God go I," may we give grace to every man we meet, and leave none without the company of our kindness.

Return to Still Pond

Winter 2001

When I was eleven years old, an exciting, new world opened to me, as it did for many young men, in the pages of the magazine *Boy's Life*. Eagerly awaited each month, it was the official publication of the Boy Scouts of America, which I had recently joined in the hope of encountering, firsthand, the rugged individualism of the Great Outdoors. In its pages I studied the adventures of other boys my age and older in places known only to my imagination. In the classifieds, I ogled ads promising to give me the body of Charles Atlas alongside photographs of men struggling to lift enormous pike taken from far-flung lakes of the North Woods—and regarded them with equal suspicion.

But dreaming of doing bold, new things and doing them are, as I would soon discover, two very different propositions. After all, I was a child of the city of Baltimore and, only recently, its greener suburbs.

I had never pitched a tent, lighted a fire, or tended to any of life's more delicate, daily necessities in anything other than civilized surroundings. These things would have to be learned, and scouting would teach me.

I have written in these pages, before, of my lifelong admiration for Dr. Carl Zapffe, the former scout master of Troop 35. The father of seven daughters, he inspired generations of boys to reach for more than what the teenage imagination, left to its own devices, might choose to pursue. But the remarkable strength of that organization and of successful scouting programs everywhere is in the example offered by the older boys. For as every parent knows, there is no surer recipe for resistance than to tell a child that this is how his father or mother thinks things should be done or—worse still— how they did them when they were his age. Let a boy discover something on his own, however, and he will learn it for life. Still Pond would be the venue for the first of many such discoveries of mine.

Nestled in a little cranny of Kent County on the Eastern Shore of Maryland, Still Pond is not a "pond" at all but a picturesque, brackish estuary of Chesapeake Bay—filled with blue crabs and surrounded by woods and farms. It emerged each summer of my boyhood as a Brigadoon of youthful activity, a Never-Never Land of swimming, sailing, canoeing, yelling, laughing and general unrest.

The pond lies just off the Sassafras River, about ten miles north of the once-sleepy fishing village of Chestertown—a place since discovered by hordes of well-heeled Washingtonians looking for the authentic, Old Bay charm. By the good offices of our scoutmaster we had secured the permission of a local farmer to overrun, for two weeks each summer, a prodigious, rolling expanse of cow pasture and woods that looked out on the pond from a bluff high above.

It was any boy's Shangri-la, this place. Well-worn trails meandered through the woods that rimmed the pasture, leading the way to an authentically rustic, timber-and-canvas "mess hall," where giant gobs of limp bacon and vats of pancakes, scrambled eggs and hash browns were served up each morning. Overlooking the pond, just west of the mess hall, was an outdoor chapel. There, with a feigned disinterest, I listened intently to one boy's father offer elegant homilies that seemed to flow directly, effortlessly from the inspiration of our surroundings. On the shore below, a wooden pier jutted some thirty yards into the water from a beach littered with the implements of adventure: long, aluminum canoes, Sunfish sailboats, and jonboats for oaring across the pond to weedbeds, where twenty or thirty white bass could be taken at a time. But it was the catfish that I preferred.

In the idle hours of many afternoons, I would stand on the outermost corner of the camp pier and cast a bait of chicken livers or whatever else was available from the kitchen. Before long there would come the telltale shudder of the line—briefly, almost imperceptibly—followed by the slow, attempted escape of an unsuspecting catfish, his movement betrayed by the line rising from the surface of the water. I learned to wait breathlessly for the line to grow taught, then set the hook with a sharp, upward heave. This method never failed to retrieve a fat, sleek specimen writhing with indignation. Taking care to avoid the knife-like, venomous, pectoral fins of the species, I would remove the hook and dash up the hill.

The camp cook had a weakness for catfish filets sautéed in butter, and he seemed more than a little bemused at the skinny boy who shared this passion. I would sometimes bring the day's victim to the back of the kitchen, where he would dress it for me. As I saw it, this ritual passed in silent recognition of my status as a "real fisherman"— not just another feckless bluegill-hunter like so many of my peers. Once, the cook spoke affectionately of what an uncommon source of strength Dr. Zapffe had been to him when

the cook's son lay dying with leukemia. He hardly needed to ask whether I knew what a special man Dr. Zapffe was. I most certainly did—all of us scouts did—with that infallible radar by which young boys everywhere are able to distinguish true leaders from pretenders. Troop 35 tried to mold young men of similar ilk, and one of the newly minted heroes was a fellow named Dave Doub.

Dave was an all-American type who would have been every mother's wish for her daughter's first date. He was certainly my mother's wish for her son's first camping trip. As the Eagle scout designated to keep me from lighting my long underwear on fire or doing myself some other serious, bodily harm on my first campout, Dave came to our apartment to sort through the odd pieces of gear that I, in my eleven-year-old's imagination, had determined might be useful. He made a few adjustments and recommendations, all the while making me feel as if I had done a remarkable job of it on my own. That first outing in the woods at Still Pond went swimmingly and, well, the rest of the story you now hold in your hands.

I returned to Still Pond last fall with my son Kip, in his 10th year. We joined Dave and Billie Roberts, who live an idyllic life in the tiny town of Still Pond, proper. When I met Dave a few years ago, I shared with him a fading memory of heading off in canoes from the scout camp to a place not far away where—impossibly, it seemed—water rushed quickly past a sand bar like a mountain stream, into the bay. A dozen of us kids had spent the afternoon, there, floating through the inlet on the swift, cool current, again and again. With time steadily fraying the picture of that day in my mind, I had come to believe it was a dream. Aging synapses, I supposed, had cross-linked my memory of some West Virginia float trip with a day of crabbing on the bay. Then, one night on a trip in the Jersey Pine Barrens, Dave heard me describe this "river" and assured me it was real. I could not have been more surprised if a shadowy lamp-merchant had just offered to take me to Aladdin's cave. Churn Creek is the very place, he explained—a narrows through which the ebb tide hurries back to the bay, near the mouth of Still Pond. We made plans to go.

Every tragic figure has a fatal flaw, and mine is the inability to resist the siren song of a small sailboat on open water. It was unthinkable, therefore, that I would come to Dave's home on the bay and not bring our little sixteen-foot sloop, *Whisper*. Kip and I resolved to *sail* to Churn Creek, like a couple of old salts. Alas, we spent a day luffing around the Sassafras River with barely a breath of wind, then anchored that night in the same place we had started. A quick meal of noodles boiled while we hunkered in the cuddy cabin had to suffice, as a passing cold front brought rain and the first chill of winter. The next morning, we decided to light out for my old scout-camp in Dave's canoe.

Paddling hard into a wind that would have been welcome in the different vessel of a day earlier, I struggled to summon the thirty-year memory of a shoreline that would reveal the location of my old camp. Eventually the familiar profile of the pier—the very altar on which so many catfish had once been sacrificed—led us in. I bolted for the hill with Kip in pursuit and Dave a distant third. At the top, the view from the bluff where the chapel had once stood was mercifully unchanged and just as inspiring, but no trace of any recent encampment was to be found. The pasture and woods were similarly preserved. We even walked to the very place where, under the tutelage of a thoughtful mentor, I first pitched a tent.

Coming to the end of camp, I looked over the open water. Dave pointed out the location of Churn Creek, but it was too far off to see. On the bay, steep whitecaps promised to stymie our passage, and winter had already begun to whisper her injunctions. The creek, I knew, would elude me for another season. It was just as well. The legends of memory had been revived. A beautiful place where I had started out, in life, had been remarkably, improbably saved. I was a happy pilgrim to my own past, and this would be a pilgrimage to be savored.

'We Few,
We Happy Few'

Winter 1995

A favorite homily familiar to many tells the story of three stone-cutters in the Middle Ages. Working side-by-side they do the same work, but each is asked in turn to describe what it is he does. The first, with his head down at his task, replies simply that he cuts rock out of the earth. The second looks slightly upward and replies that he shapes rock into a form suitable for building. The third puts down his tools, raises his eyes to the heavens, and with a swell of pride exclaims that he is building a great cathedral.

Perspective to see the passage of time and the slow march of ordinary events across a larger canvas is an elusive and rare talent. Kings and princes have paid handsomely for it, for centuries. It is aided neither by intelligence nor education nor wealth nor status, but in the solitude and simple pace of wilderness it seems often to reveal itself. Rarely have I come back from even the most abysmal, rain-soaked misadventure in the wild without some sense of a needed course-correction or a renewed understanding of the reasons to press on.

It is clearly not only great fun to run rivers and explore wild places but instructive, as well, to re-encounter what life is like away from the din of civilized society. In that moment when we stand in a silent woods or beside a still lake, with nothing to keep us company but our thoughts and one another, and nothing to *do* but take in the world around us, we taste something of the essence of man's life on earth that has not changed across the millennia. We may pine for the comforts of modernity, but there are lessons to be learned in the starkness of nature that cannot be captured in the glow of our television sets. Among these are the lost art of conversation, the meditations of solitude, and a sense of our own insignificance in the larger order of things.

The rivers and lakes we paddle were here thousands of years before us, and they will remain thousands of years after we are gone. A mere hundred years after these words are written, none who read them now will walk this earth. If each of us is not by his daily labor building a cathedral somewhere in his own life, to what purpose do we work at all?

I came to ask that question of myself one day four years ago in Houston. In my mid-thirties, I had been cutting rocks steadily for ten years since entering law school, with no cathedral in sight. I was at an age and a point in my career when most lawyers were looking to move up to that *big* house, with the really *big* mortgage, followed in due course by longer hours at the office, the *big* ulcer, the twelve-step recovery program, and the rebellion of lonely children who never really became a priority in their parents' schedule. As the birth of my little daughter Caroline approached, there came an impending sense that life really is not a dress rehearsal, that one doesn't get a

second chance to better raise one's children, or to be young and healthy, or to make the kinds of mistakes and try out the wild-eyed dreams that are forbidden to us in the frailty of old age. And so I sold our Texas law practice, took off for North Carolina, opened and failed in a sailboat-charter business, and later re-opened a smaller law office. Here in the piney woods, the grand experiment of which this journal is a product continues.

Part of that experiment has happily been more time spent along the rivers and ponds depicted in this issue. These places and others to be covered in the seasons ahead offer an interesting contradiction to conventional wisdom. Expecting to find crowds of people in many wild places within a short driving distance of large cities, I have more often than not found ourselves alone in the woods, or nearly so. While many state and national parks are jammed with crowds of tourists of the worst ilk and overrun by day hikers, there seems to be less if not little competition—knock on wood—for the primitive campsites along canoe trails.

Some theorize that the rise of the two-earner household and the difficulty of coordinating an extended vacation for two workers at once has confined most of us to venues accessible within the time-span of a weekend. Travel experts have cited a trend toward shorter, two to five-day vacations. There are other explanations, too. Many would say that we have seen a growing

crassness in a public which seems increasingly less in tune with what came to be coined in the 1970's as the "wilderness experience." Witness today the incessant whine of personal ski-boats circling like so many flies on the water, and how infrequently one sees a canoe gliding by. In his book *Canoeing the Jersey Pine Barrens*, Robert Parnes wrote that "camping is not the same as it used to be. There are more people, and campers are more wasteful, leaving behind unwanted belongings, trash, and unsightly campfire pits." He is right—but elsewhere, on the game lands, in the national forests, and along established water trails, there is refuge. The key is finding those places where the facilities are primitive and the access is limited, which is every canoe tripper's itinerary.

Two years ago, when planning a trip along the most storied canoe route of the Adirondacks in the height of the summer season, I was warned that vacant campsites would be few and far between. Instead, I found that few sites were occupied, and those people I did see were quiet and respectful folk.   The same experience has been repeated elsewhere, including the rivers and creeks of the Croatan covered in this issue.   There are pockets of wilderness everywhere.   With the native people of this land long since displaced and the rest of America having safely retreated to the suburbs, who can say that on any given Wednesday afternoon in October you might not have the lake you paddle more to yourself than did the earliest explorers of our age?

Whatever the reason, those today who take to the wild by simple means, seeking simple pleasures, are clearly few in number.   Let millions build an altar to MTV and the myriad distractions of modern life, but "we few, we happy few" can, with pack and paddle in hand, yet find that quiet, uncluttered exuberance which the poet promised us along the road less traveled.

What, Me Worry?

Spring 2001

I have long been a hater of cell phones. It is true there was a time, when these devices first appeared on the market, when this was not the case. I was frantically trying to manage some semblance of a life apart from our law practice in Houston, in the late 1980's, and I carried a bulky apparatus (we called them "car phones" back then) similar to what the president now keeps at hand for launching global, thermonuclear war. But for me, the bloom fell off the car-phone rose long ago. Readers of this journal know well the story of the (early) middle-age jitters that led me to abandon that fast-paced life and all of its symbols, including incessant, compulsive yakking on cell phones. ("Hello, Honey. I just wanted you to know that since pulling out of the driveway thirty seconds ago, I arrived at the end of the street and all is well. How's everything at home?") The latest technology be damned, I say! But as I would come to learn, technology is a jealous mistress.

It was to be just a quick trip in late March—a weekend jaunt on Antietam Creek on the Maryland side of the Potomac River. The weather had turned favorably warmer the weekend before and, seeing a window of opportunity open, I decided on short notice to make the five-hour drive north to complete the trip featured in this issue. My daughter Caroline would join me for the drive as far as her cousin Emma's house in Silver Spring, Maryland.

A cold rain was falling as I drove the final 50 miles early Saturday morning from Silver Spring to Boonsboro. When throwing together the plans for this trip three nights before, I had found the web page of the local canoe-outfitter and the announcement that he would open for the season on the Saturday morning I would arrive. With the bliss that is ignorance, I expected to arrange a shuttle when I got there. You can write the next line in this tale, no doubt.

I arrived at Devil's Backbone County Park in Boonsboro and stopped a kayaker making plans for the day's paddle. The fact that he was donning a wet suit at the time, as protection against cold-water immersion, was not lost on me in my long woolies.

"Do you know where the canoe-rental place is?" I asked. He pointed to a barn just across the street, on the bank of the river below the bridge. Other than a trailer full of canoes, there was no sign of the outfitter. It was ten o'clock in the morning, and another window of opportunity—enough daylight to complete the thirteen-mile paddle to the campground at the

C & O Canal National Historic Park—was rapidly closing. I could have called the outfitter easily enough had there been a payphone at the park, but "easy" is a word not often associated with the trips I make for this journal. Instead I hopped in my boat and paddled off under the assumption that I would find a payphone downriver at the National Park Service campground, from which to summon the 82nd Airborne, if need be, to fetch me back to my car.

Part of being male is a physiological predisposition against fretting and worrying. As every wife knows, being a man is to live in an all-is-well, don't-worry-be-happy, let-the-devil-take-tomorrow, if-I-ignore-that-clicking-sound-it-will-probably-go-away, state of mind. I like being a guy for this reason. My wife frets and worries far more than I do. She would have fretted and worried about making contact with the outfitter all the way down the river. No, she would have turned around and driven straight home before heading off on the assumption that she would later somehow reach a person who could bring her back to her car. No, in fact, a hundred other worries would have kept her away from a cold, Western Maryland creek on a rainy day in the first place.

Worries rarely intrude on a man's thoughts until there is no longer anything he can do about them. By this time, they are more accurately described as "regrets." Women may worry, but men have lots of regrets. Woman: "Shouldn't we look at the map, Dear, before we make this turn?" Man (two hours later): "I now *regret* that I didn't look at the map, Dear, *before* we drove one hundred miles in the wrong direction and missed your sister's wedding, but I was never *worried*."

My regrets on this trip started early. Upon encountering the first haystack in the chilly, not-quite-yet-in-season water of the Antietam, I realized I had not had the benefit of speaking to a live person about where the rapids are, how to run them, or whether I had any business at all being on this river alone, in late March. Then again, years of paddling dozens of rivers and hundreds of haystacks just like this one had taught me a thing or two, by golly, and I surfed the first ledge in fine form. Four hours later, I washed out into the Potomac and found the landing that leads to the campground. Life was good.

Coming up the bank to the towpath, I asked a day-hiker whether there was a phone nearby. "No," he said, "but you're

welcome to use my cell
phone." To my amazement,
he pulled one right out of
his pocket. I used it to call
my sister-in-law in Silver
Spring. "I am at the
Antietam Creek Ranger
Station," I explained to
Susan as I stood on the
towpath reading a sign with
those very words. "Call the
outfitter and tell him he can
pick me up here anytime
tomorrow morning, and
don't worry." I must say I
now *regret* not knowing, at
the time, that the ranger
station had recently been
removed from the towpath,
where the campground is
located, and that the only
ranger station in the area
was four miles away, in
Sharpsburg.

After an enjoyable
evening camped alone above
the banks of the Potomac—
the only camper there—I
allowed myself the luxury of
sleeping late on a chilly,
Sunday morning. Outside
my bivouac I could hear the
voices of day-trippers and
kayakers assembling for the
day to surf Furnace Rapids.

Fearing this might be my last chance for a phone call, I importuned one of them to let me use his cell phone. ("It's just a local call—would you mind, terribly?") I reached my brother-in-law Michael, who was surprised to hear that the outfitter was not there. Michael promised to find out what happened, but the kayakers left for the river, and I was unable to call him back. I returned to my phone-less campsite and waited, not knowing that the outfitter would report to my family that he had arrived at "the ranger station" as instructed, long ago, and found no sign of me.

The morning waned into afternoon as I waited resolutely in camp, heaping one log after another onto what, after several hours, had become the perfect campfire for roasting a small buffalo. The volunteer campground-host who had chatted with me the night before about wood-canvas canoes began to worry as the sky threatened rain. He offered to drive me back to my Jeep. I accepted, doused the fire, and left camp. Unbeknownst to me, the outfitter not ten minutes later would find my "abandoned" camp beside the towpath and, with growing alarm, alert the park service to a missing person named Mike Hurley. Maintaining steady contact with my sister-in-law on his cell phone, the outfitter assured her that he found "no sign of a struggle" at my camp. Knowing that he had even thought to look for such a sign brought tears of worry to Susan, who wondered if I had met my doom on the Antietam.

Returning in my Jeep to break camp, I finally met the beleaguered owner of Antietam Creek Canoes, who refused my offers to pay for the shuttle. A young ranger stopped to ask my name, picked up her radio mike, and called off the search for the missing canoeist. When I got home, several plans for a cell-phone contract were waiting for my perusal. Never mind running from your past—the future will catch up with you a lot quicker.

Nowadays I am never without my little gray friend, but I worry more. I worry that my battery either is not charged or is not achieving its true potential. I worry that messages I would have let languish on my office voicemail might be too urgent to wait until the next morning, and so I call—twice a day. I worry that my wife will worry if I don't call, and so I do. I worry that I am spending $59.95 a month for something that, if the truth be told, I will really *need* only once a year. As I write this, a blinking green light signals that a cell tower, somewhere, knows where I am. No outfitter in North America is beyond my reach, and it seems the wilderness just got a little smaller. Call me anytime. I'll worry if you don't.

On Solitude

Summer 2001

O ne of the unexpected lessons of this journal for
me, as its creator, has revolved around the
discipline of solitude. Having only recently
enlisted the aid of contributing editors for the stories you
read in these pages, for six years I have had the privilege
and duty to travel to various parts of this country, making
upwards of eight or nine trips each season to feature in
the journal. The tyranny of the deadline often forced me
to go at times when school or family schedules did not
permit the company of my wife and children. Many of
you may travel on business in circumstances where
colleagues, airline stewards, and hotel clerks maintain at
least a veneer of those relationships we call "society." It is
quite another thing to leave behind both the comforts of
home and the companionship of other human beings to
enter a wilderness, alone. What is it like, you may
wonder, to load one's provisions and shove off into a
speechless void for days at a time? I am a family man and

no advocate of the hermit's life, but I have found an unexpected virtue in the occasional necessity of solitude.

Sigurd Olson was said to possess a "wilderness within," and that is certainly a concept I have come to identify in my own life. Incidentally, those who grieve for the glory of this country's unspoiled frontier can find a reasonable facsimile of the pioneer experience surprisingly close at hand, when they paddle solo. I have been as desolately and completely alone on tiny streams not five miles from a major city as I have been on distant, windswept lakes in the Boundary Waters. My most surprising discoveries on these trips have come in the mental wilderness, not from my physical surroundings.

If you could sift from life all of its frenzy and detail as one might sift gold from sand, the gift of solitude would be among the treasures that remained. Entering the woods alone reduces daily life to an elemental level we scarcely recognize amid the traffic, television, appliances, and architecture of modern man. Seeing it for the first time through the door of a tent in a soft, lingering rain can be unsettling. In similar conditions at home, we might seek the narcotic effects of television to fill the hours and spare us the burden of creative imagination. Whether the solitary experience of wilderness becomes an ordeal or an epiphany depends on one's approach and perspective.

I had set out for a week alone on the Canadian border, one summer, when I encountered a large family traveling together. The children were thrilled to be free to swim and race around the woods while mom and dad lagged tiredly behind. I paddled not far from their camp, trolling for walleye for dinner and enjoying the excited shouts and antics of the children. The man noticed that I was alone and, with a wistful look, remarked at how I must be enjoying the solitude in such a place. Just then, though, I had been imagining how much more I would have enjoyed playing with my own children and talking with my wife in that very spot. Two days later, I passed a young couple who had pitched their tent on a small lake they had all to themselves. They were enjoying a veritable Garden of Eden, without a stitch of clothing between them. As I kept paddling so as not to disturb their paradise, I was reminded, again, of the companion I had left home. What fish I caught on that trip were mine alone to admire, and what wonders I saw it was pointless to exclaim. No one could hear me. After awhile, an undisciplined mind in that circumstance will—as goes the song about Camp Grenada—begin to be more acutely aware of life's difficulties and less acutely aware of life's beauty. We are social creatures, to be sure. That being so, there is a natural temptation to despair in being alone, but the greater pity is to give in to despair and let that obscure the lessons that solitude offers.

The tradition of my Catholic faith is one of contemplation and reflection. We are constantly urged to repair to some quiet place to better discern the divine will, and we are reminded that Christ often did the same—in preparation for times of trial and uncertainty. The truth is that many who speak enthusiastically of their time in the "wilderness" actually never experience the rejuvenation it offers. A group of drinking buddies off for a week in the woods has merely taken a form of social interaction that might otherwise have occurred at a ballpark and improved the scenery a bit. That can be great fun, of course, but the hidden gift of wilderness is introspection. It is a cathedral created by God to bring us closer to him through a better knowledge of ourselves. Solitude accelerates the process of self-discovery by simplifying life's routine and reducing the number of demands on our senses.

There is no wilderness on earth so isolated as the sea, nor any the contours of which remain as unchanged by time and man. You can get a sense of that isolation in the story of Assateague Island, in this issue. Not far from that coast, my wife and children and I were very much "together" in the cramped space of a small sailboat for three days, this summer. We wended our

way from the charming and historic town of St. Michael's, on the Eastern Shore of Maryland, to the equally charming and historic town of Annapolis. At night we lay at anchor on a huge air mattress in the cockpit, staring up at the moon and stars. We giggled uncontrollably when unexpected winds rocked the boat—tossing us around on the mattress like a trampoline. I felt a surge of pride when we sailed past the Thomas Point Lighthouse in Chesapeake Bay, and I called the children out to make sure they witnessed the moment. Later that day, after we had dropped anchor in Annapolis Harbor, we strolled proudly down the streets of the city like Magellan and his crew in the South Pacific. I pointed out historic paintings of the Thomas Point Light to Julie and the children. Seeing these sealed our collective memory that "We were there—together!" It would not have meant as much to me to have rounded that mark alone.

The plan for the remainder of this summer trip was for Julie and our children to see her sister's family while my brother-in-law joined me for the twenty-two mile sail between Annapolis and Baltimore's Inner Harbor. It had been my dream since I was a child to sail my own boat into the harbor where I was born. When my brother-in-law had to cancel at the last minute, I resolved to make the trip alone. Sailing a quiet ship was a distinct contrast to the preceding days full of conversation, laughter, and shared adventure. Then again, running against a gathering thunderstorm to find a tiny cove depicted on the chart, anchoring there in the moist, summer evening, and watching in silence as a storm of apocalyptic proportions passed over the bay were solitary experiences I will never forget. That I relished this interlude is no slight to the wonderful time I had with my family. The virtue I try to make from the necessity of solitude is an appreciation for each experience in life—realizing that the opportunity for that experience will soon pass, perhaps never to return.

In May of this year I celebrated twenty years of marriage to my college sweetheart. At 43, I am not far from that meridian past which the majority of my time on this earth will have been spent as someone's partner. It may seem strange in the afterglow of this milestone to ponder the subject of solitude, but marriage has taught me the importance of the individual. It takes a whole person to make half a marriage.

It was after sundown before I reached the inner harbor. When I arrived, the evening breeze was all but calm. My sails billowed only slightly, allowing me to cruise slowly enough to discover an unexpected anchorage right in the middle of the city. My little ship was one of only four boats anchored amid the spectacular display. The entire harbor was decorated in white lights. Paddle boats in the shape of sea monsters ghosted quietly about in the twilight, adding a dreamlike quality. Roots music from an outdoor concert drifted over the water, and it seemed as if I had suddenly arrived on another continent. "You can't believe how beautiful it is," I told my wife on the phone. "I'll be there tomorrow," she replied. We met the next morning like two young lovers on the docks, below the stern of a great sailing ship, and I showed her all the wonders I had found.

Neither a recluse nor a clinging vine will I be. For every one of life's treasures there is a season. What solitude invites us to discover, our hearts compel us to share.

Breaking Camp

Fall 1997

As I poked at the embers on a midsummer evening, this year, a familiar companion emerged from the shadows and took his seat at the campfire beside me. It was the end of a glorious week in the wilds of Canada, near the end of a glorious season spent in many such venues on many evenings beside many campfires. But his entrance was not entirely unexpected. He seems to happen by at about the same time, every year. Whether we're standing on an ocean beach or perched on a rocky crag in the woods, he passes over many of us like a sudden change in the weather. The woods and waters never lose their luster, and the dawn may still sing its hallelujahs, but there slowly comes a difference in us. I'm talking about that old Puritan anxiety, that back-to-school, down-to-business, what-am-I-doing-here-skipping-rocks-when-I've-got-work-to-do feeling that, try as we may, seems to be an inescapable appendage of the civilized psyche.

I am best acquainted with this emotion as it manifests itself in the waning days of a canoe trip. In children it is called homesickness, but as an adult with family, friends, and all the best parts of

"home" gathered about me in the wild, it is something different altogether. It wells up from a campfire when the food pack finally lifts a little lighter and no more grand, culinary ambitions drive our efforts at the wood pile. It is the force that pauses the fisherman's hand upon the rod, once undeterred but now content to settle into the grain of the paddle on a steadier, homeward course. Rocks and pools that invited "just one more cast" at the start of the journey now slide by under an admiring but unstudied

glance. Standing on the shore we cast our eyes farther into the distance than before, seeing neither the lake nor the river nor the trees but something out on the horizon of our lives: what will be, what remains to be done, what challenge awaits, what test is to be met, what greater purpose is to be answered. It is that familiar feeling of breaking camp—tinged less with sadness than with resolve and renewed purpose to shape our lives.

This is both the blessing and the curse of Modern Man. So many of those things that intrigue us and bring such challenge and excitement to our world—art, science, literature, theater, enterprise—derive from urban, social interaction. I have come to understand that this is precisely why wilderness, with its perfect simplicity of physical structure and predictable rituals of daily activity, offers the urban animal such an oasis. An oasis is by definition a thing of contrast, and without contrast it loses its meaning and preciousness.

In the fat happiness of July, my friend Tom Tompkins and I had wandered from our canoe near the ruins of Hazard Mill, on the South Fork of the Shenandoah River. We were searching half-heartedly for the reported location of an ancient Indian village recently unearthed by archaeologists. Not finding any sign or artifact of the encampment, and growing apprehensive of the poison ivy round about our ankles, we resolved to head back to the canoe and continue our journey homeward. As we began, Tom posed a question: "Could you have lived like that?" he asked, referring to the lives of the Indians of whom we had found no evidence. We had fed ourselves to overfilling with fish from this river only the night before and had landed by canoe at a primitive camp in the woods, so it seemed to me at first that "living like that" was exactly what we had been doing for the past two days. But I had misunderstood his question, and he explained further: "I mean living in the woods permanently—making all of your tools, hunting and gathering all of your food, day in and day out, month after month, year after year."

I paused a while before answering Tom's question, as it was squarely one that I have considered, yet never resolved to my satisfaction, on every occasion I have gone into the woods. No matter how beautiful the surroundings, how glorious the fishing, or how fair the weather, there comes a point at which the isolation we once so highly prized becomes a source of small but undeniable concern for the routines we have left behind. The

campfire on the last night of the trip burns never so brightly as on the first, and our sleep is never so free and easy as on those nights when we have just begun the voyage.

Most of us I would guess have had this emotion. It is perhaps the biological prompting of our ancestors, stored in our genes to wake us from the dangers of complacency. It stirs us in the lush of summer to remember and prepare for the lean of fall. It is the same feeling which, though it may hang like a pall over the gaiety of sun-kissed afternoons, still promises to invigorate us with the duties of autumn—school and studies, harvest time, putting up stores against the winter, and a return to the discipline of life indoors.

A child of postwar, suburban America, I am no foundling of the wilderness by any means. Long unseen family members who read this journal and recall my teenage years spent in the thrall of jazz piano and politics must wonder whether I have since resolved to quit civilization for life in a canoe. On the contrary, it is precisely the accoutrements of civilization that bring to the wilderness experience that depth of contrast which gives it clearer meaning and importance. Were it not for our urbanity, would there even be such a notion as "wilderness"?

Native peoples, it seemed, lacked the distraction and shortened attention span of modern life. To them the woods were home. George Washington Sears, the Adirondack explorer known as "Nessmuk," observed in 1880 that an Indian baby "is not expensive in the way of playthings" and would sit "placidly content" for hours "gazing at the mysteries of the forest." We children of the modern world it seems are conditioned to require more varied and frequent stimuli.

Years ago on one fall afternoon, I felt compelled to gas up a battered VW wagon and chitty-bang my way with axe and saw up to the Catoctin Mountains of Maryland, near Thurmont. Under a cloudless, blue sky tinged with the cool portent of winter, I labored until I had gathered and split a trunkload of firewood; then I lay back amidst the clean smell of wool, sweat, and pine to soak up what I feared might be the last, hospitable afternoon of the season. It was fitting work to be done on such a halcyon day. But as I lay there my thoughts wandered on—to apple-cider stands by the roadside, to the smell of pigskin and parties on crisp, dry leaves, to the jazz and ambiance of the King of France Tavern, to Thanksgiving feasts and bundled shoppers on city streets, and to the place where the wood at my feet would warm us. I hurried home.

Let us likewise make glad haste again in this fall season to break camp. Better for the journey and with a spring in our stroke we shall paddle home—home to the towns, halls, schools, and hubbub of modern life from whence the wilderness learns anew its precious worth.

A Perfect World

Fall 2001

I spent the week before September 11 in a perfect world, and I had hoped to celebrate it with you, now, in this column. It was and is a world of wilderness along the Grass River, in New York. It is a place in kind and character familiar to most of you. In paddling through it I was struck as I often am, in such places, by the unfailing perfection of God's creation. Rivers like these run endlessly through the ages. Fish thrive, grasses grow redolent with blossoms, and trees find root and prosper. Seasons come and go in an infinite cycle of birth, decay, and renewal. Nothing lives or dies in the woods without a purpose. No life is taken in vain. There are no terrorists, here.

Each creature in the wild does exactly what God created it to do, which is to say it does exactly and only what is necessary to survive and ensure the survival of the whole. The wilderness presents a remarkable theorem of life that we cannot comprehend in its infinite details but which is infallibly proved again and again with each new dawn. The wilderness is, indeed, a perfect world. It is a place very different from the one to which I returned on September 11. And the story I had hoped to tell you of that world seems to pale in irrelevance to the one in which we all live. Ours is a supremely imperfect world, and the history of it is sobering to contemplate.

It is a tale of a hundred woes and a thousand sorrows. It is the story of a child who has lost a father, a mother who has lost a son, and a man who has lost hope at the bottom of a bottle. It is a story of the cross, the tomb, the valley, and the abyss of despair. It is a tale of betrayals—of trust gained and broken, of unspeakable grief, of divorce and death, of lives ruined and lives wasted. It is a story of world wars, of madmen and heroes, of unfathomable cruelty amidst inexplicable mercy. It is a story of Antietam, Auschwitz, Iwo Jima and Pelilu, of the frozen Chosin and Kesahn, of Waco and Columbine, of the seventh of December, the twenty-second of November, and now the eleventh of September. It is the story of us. It is the story of this world as it has been, is now, and ever shall be.

I have been thinking a lot, lately, of that familiar Bible passage in which Jesus, having languished in the desert for forty days and nights, is taken by Satan to the mountaintop and given a vision of all the kingdoms of the earth. Jesus was tempted, we are told, to exchange his divinity for the opportunity of an earthly kingship—an offer he refused in order to purchase, with his body and blood, a heavenly kingdom for us all.

To those of you who do not share the Christian faith, I mean no offense by these remarks. In moments of deepest doubt, we simply have no comfort or counsel to offer beyond what our own faith supplies. And by faith I believe that Satan's offer and Christ's refusal in the desert two thousand years ago provides us the perspective to understand what is happening in the deserts of Afghanistan, today.

156

What fascinates me about the Bible story of this encounter between Good and Evil is that the gospel writers who tell it speak of Jesus being *tempted*. Imagine that for a moment. It seems almost blasphemous to ascribe to Christ the uniquely human capacity for temptation, but his life without sin would be meaningless without that capacity. He was, I believe, both utterly human and utterly divine. Temptation implies a desire for that which we do not have, as temptation cannot exist without desire. What, then, could possibly have been *tempting* to Jesus? This was not a man whose life was marked by an interest in money or material possessions or political power. Indeed, he led his disciples in headlong retreat from those ideals. One does not imagine that all of the gold or jewels or wealth of the world would have held any attraction for him—he would have seen the transience of all such things. What could Satan possibly have offered Jesus that Jesus did not have but valued and desired?

I imagine that what Satan showed Jesus in an instant on the mountaintop were not the riches of the world but the sorrows it would endure. I believe he saw, in that moment, the horrors of the Inquisition, the carnage of the Civil War, and the ravages of Hitler and Hirohito. I believe he saw the suffering of all disease and injury and the defilement of God's creation. I believe he saw the sorrows and pain that every one of us will face on the way to the grave, and I believe he saw the jets of September 11. If there was temptation in that moment for Jesus, it surely must have been not the desire to rule creation but to preserve it—to exchange his Father's heavenly paradise for an earthly one; to be our king on this earth and walk among us down through the centuries, to save us the pain of war, to heal not just the sick and lame of Galilee and Judea but all mankind of every affliction for all time. His temptation must surely have been to use the power that was awakening within him to alleviate the present, physical suffering of the world, but the price Satan demanded was nothing less than Christ himself—the very ransom for our souls. And in the choice Jesus made we find not only our salvation but a lesson for the world in which we now live.

The human experience in this life will always be an imperfect story. That is the fundamental reality of this world and our time within it. Understand this when you see a child born with cerebral palsy, a young boy called to die for the cause of freedom, or a plane fly into a building full of people. We did not wake up on September 11 to a suddenly imperfect, often cruel and dangerous world. It has been so since the Fall of Man. But in our struggle against this latest enemy, we should not delude ourselves that we will ever find peace in mere physical safety or that the greatest dangers we face are from men who lurk in shadowy caves a world away.

What insight do our own travels in the wilderness offer us in this crisis? Perhaps, as Jesus did, we will find something eternal, there—something that affirms the divine spirit within all of us.

I remember standing with my son Kip, several years ago, at a scout camp. It was the first, big camping trip for many of the boys, and there were the usual fears to soothe about bogeymen in the woods. As the leader spoke, I found my eyes drifting to the distant forest. At first I noticed how foreboding it must have seemed to the boys—the trees densely drawn together almost as a curtain, hiding a dangerous, unknown beyond. Then I noticed something in myself. I recognized an impulse to explore deep within those woods and realized that I felt none of the anxiety of being alone in a dark forest that most folks—my wife chief among them—would consider part of being "normal." In fact, I rarely feel as safe and sanguine as when I am utterly isolated in the wild. There is something in the wilderness—a sense of order, a fleeting image of the divine—that touches someplace deep within all of us. It speaks to a part of our souls that remembers who God is and yearns to see his face. It clears

our mind and clarifies our choices. I suppose that is why, when I heard of the fourth plane on September 11 and wondered where the next strike would come, my mind wandered again to the edge of the forest.

When I think of safety, I think of a night beneath the stars, beside a waterfall in a river full of trout, and the dancing flames of a campfire. I think of my bare feet resting in a spot on the forest floor where the sun breaks through on a fall afternoon and warms the pine needles like toast. I think of thoroughfares that know no roads or runways or engines, where only boots and paddles can take you. I think of a perfect world, and I know that the world to which we must all return will never be so comforting.

It is well we should strive for Peace on Earth. That is, after all, the Great Commission. We in the United States have come closer to fulfilling that commission than any nation in history, but in this world it will always elude us. It is well we should strive to cure disease and ease suffering, but in this world man will die. It is well we should defend our families and our country, and may God have mercy on the souls of those who compel us to that task. But let us never forget that there remains a fate worse than death and a goal higher than our personal safety. Peace be with you, my friend, and peace be with our enemies. May you savor each day in this imperfect world and never lose hope for the perfection of the world to come.

Time and Tide

Winter 2002

Pulling onto Interstate 95 in the early morning
hours, I looked for my place in the caravan of
pilgrims heading south. We were on a journey to
Mecca, all of us—strangers bound together by a ribbon
of asphalt, rifling at a steady speed toward the warm,
Florida sunshine. License plates from distant lands told
the tale. We all hoped to find a few days of respite from
the drear and humdrum days of work and darkness
farther north. We would go and gather in our time in
the coming days like wheat, carefully savoring each
moment and storing it away to feed our souls during the
winter ahead.

Staring at the fleeing horizon of the highway, I
kept up a steely indifference to the passage of time,
looking neither to the right nor the left nor, for that
matter, at what lay ahead. I could see the road well
enough, but I was gazing more inside myself, toward a

horizon of memory. Suddenly it was 1978, again, and I was a twenty-year old officer candidate at the Marine Corps base in Quantico. In the hot, Virginia sun, the smell of freshly mowed grass mixed with the odor of tar melting on the tarmac beneath our boots. I stood with my platoon of an unlikely mix of college boys in starchy, new fatigues. The temperature rose to eighty, then eighty-five. Later that day, during drills, a black flag would rise above the base that would send us to our barracks for the afternoon—there to polish belt buckles and boots to an astonishing brilliance—but for now we stood erect and still in the gathering warmth.

The drill sergeant passed by our line slowly, menacingly, like a barracuda circling a reef. He was younger than the gunny whom we most feared, and he lacked that authentically callous manner of a seasoned marine, but he carried the same authority over us. Coming to me, he paused, and I stiffened what few muscles that were not already locked in readiness. You never looked at him. Never. You stared ahead. You stared inside. You stared past the present moment. You stared at a mental

image of your girlfriend on the distant tarmac, but never at him.
A credit card emerged from his pocket, and he swiped it across
my chin. It made an incriminating noise. He moved closer to
speak to me—so close I could have seen every follicle in his jaw,
as clean and close as a baby's bottom. I had been shaving in
earnest for only three years, then, but I had not done so that
morning—there hadn't been *time*.

Time was the real luxury in this place, and a drill
instructor has a special talent both to suspend and accelerate the
movement of it. He awakened us shortly after four o'clock each
morning, just a few short hours—it seemed like seconds,
really—after we hit the rack. No sooner had our feet touched
the floor than we were running out of time to shower, shave and
dress. I had skipped the shaving that morning, hoping that my
anemic beard would not betray me so easily. I was wrong, and
in the years since I have become much more accomplished at the
quick shave. But in those days, at that place in memory, *time*
was an unforgiving master.

In the classroom that afternoon, an M-16 rifle lay on the
desk before each man, as it had every day before. A stopwatch
in the hand of a special forces expert at the head of the room
lorded over all of us. "Click," he pressed the watch, and we
began the hurried work of disassembling the pieces of the M-16
and arranging them all neatly on the desk. "Click," and we
made the weapon whole again. "Click," and we did it still faster
the next time. I was fast. I was very fast. And when the captain
sent the whole platoon on a long-distance run, I made it back to
base ahead of the pack—*way ahead*. The physical part of OCS
was a cakewalk compared to my experience on the track and
lacrosse teams, but in officer candidate school, the compression
of time and the constraints on the freedom of a self-absorbed
twenty-year old are a powerful voodoo. Stupidly, I left the
program, electing not to return the following summer and
abandoning the prize of a commission as a second lieutenant.

Whether I would have made a good marine or even had any business applying for the job are open and exceedingly unimportant questions, now. All I can say is that there are three moments in my life that I would like to have back, and one is the day when I walked away from Quantico. All three have in common a failure to master the tyranny of my own impatience and the inability to imagine what lay beyond a given point in time.

What I have learned since those younger days is that we do not pass through life—life passes through us at a steady and predictable rhythm, like a tide. We must have the patience to wait for its arrival and the wisdom to act at the fullness of the swell. On its flood ride life's opportunities. With its ebb go the choices we make. Some moments of decision return to us for further deliberation, others are swept out to sea, gone forever in an instant.

Four hours flew by almost imperceptibly, and a tiny yellow light began to glow from my dashboard somewhere in southern Georgia. I needed gas. At one of those endearingly tacky, roadside shops off of Interstate 95, I noticed an empty can of "Florida Sunshine" for sale next to the rows of pecan divinity. I wouldn't need a can, I thought. The sunshine where I was going would be stored in memory for decades to come.

Arriving at the last toll booth before Key Largo, I switched the radio dial to a lively, Cuban station. Hearing Spanish spoken fluently for the first time in a long while, I could scarcely understand it. A succession of power poles raced past my headlights in the darkness of the Keys Highway. Eager vacationers crowded my bumper, but signs cleverly spaced in single file along the shoulder offered these words of encouragement. "Patience . . . pays . . . Only . . . three . . . miles . . . to . . . next . . . passing . . . zone." As a singer on the radio crooned, "Tu eres el mejor," I recalled my first, halting efforts to

learn the language in Puerto Rico in the summer of '72, from the dog-eared pages of a Spanish-English dictionary.

My old Jeep finally rattled to a stop in front of the Caribbean Club in Key Largo at midnight. Though dawn came early the next morning, I had no complaint. My kayak eased forward, and the waters of Florida Bay bubbled up around my waist—warmer than I had expected. A steady thrust of the paddle divided the unfettered hours into a purposeful rhythm. I passed an entire family fishing from a boat anchored in the inlet. The ebb tide swirled around their transom and fled seaward. A gray-haired grandmother, easily in her eighties, stared silently at a thin line of monofilament that disappeared beneath the mangroves. I coasted past them effortlessly on a flying ribbon of green water.

When I finally drifted into the pale-blue shallows of North Nest Key, I saw no one at first. Then, rounding the southern tip of the island, I encountered a man and his wife fishing from a boat. They were surprised to see me in this deserted place. The woman hurriedly pulled a towel over herself but then, concluding that I posed no danger, resumed her worship of the setting sun. Later, I saw their boat fade into the distance as I pitched my tent on the sand. Storm clouds gathered far away in the gulf.

That evening, rain and wind roared across the tiny, emerald strands that lie scattered along this turquoise sea. With nowhere to go on my island home, I relished several hours of unplanned rest and introspection. At midnight, when it seemed as if the wind might lift up my bivouac and hurl it into the mangroves, I wondered if my stay might be prolonged. I had little food but plenty of water and, certainly, no cause for worry. The air of the storm was balmy and sweet. The sand was harder than expected, but I was not anxious for sleep. Somewhere in the twilight, between my thoughts and my dreams, it occurred to me that time has taken on a warmer hue with the passing years. All but gone, now, is the impetuous boy I once knew. I have come to find, in places of quiet solitude like this, a recompense for the haste of my adolescence and the hope of wisdom in my old age. Time and tide, it is said, waits for no man—but the wise man waits for the tide.

Dawn brought blue skies and fair winds to my camp on North Nest Key. In my kayak again, I was born softly off the sands by gentle waves. A blister in my hand, unaccustomed to the turn of the double paddle, stung slightly in the salt water, but it would heal. So too will all hearts, with time. I paused awhile beside the mangroves to rest. It was good to feel the sunshine. It was good to wait, in this place. The tide had changed, and so had I.

A Young Man's Fancy

Spring 2002

I await the spring eagerly every year now, just as I did as a boy. Back in those days, when I lived in Maryland's northern counties above Baltimore, my winter penance sometimes would not fully subside until mid May. Before then, the fishing and everything else that one might plan for a day in the outdoors was shrouded in doubt for what tantrums the weather gods might throw our way.

In every place I have lived, from St. Louis to Houston to the coast of North Carolina, I have heard the locals describe their climate by the phrase, "If you don't like the weather around here, wait a minute." But Baltimore, nestled between the Chesapeake Bay to the south and east and the Pocono and Appalachian Mountains to the north and west, truly lives up to that reputation. It is a reputation never better deserved than in the springtime.

Unlike my peers, in the spring of my sixteenth year I had very little interest—well, no interest, really—in the usual objects of what Lord Tennyson so aptly described as a "young man's fancy." My fancy then was the rise of a trout and the slow approach of a largemouth bass. In fact, when my sixteenth birthday arrived I didn't know how to dance or drive a car. I hadn't even bothered to get a driver's license; there was no need. Shepard Pratt Pond was an easy bike ride from my house and a short walk from the home of my pal Barry Skinner. The Shepard Pratt estate had long ago been turned into a mental-health institution. Happily, its sweeping pastures and woods had been preserved for the relaxation of its

patients and the trespassory adventures of kids in the neighborhood who knew the pond's secret: bass. Big bass. You could fish all season at Loch Raven Reservoir out in the county and never come across lunkers like those hiding under the great, fallen tree that stretched halfway across the dark water of the pond. Branches fingered out into the murky depths, offering excellent hiding places for the swarms of fingerlings that would swiftly grow to impressive size.

A Young Man's Fancy

The first book I ever wrote was a pamphlet I published myself at the age of 13 or so, entitled "A 101 Ways to Better Your Bass Fishing." Whatever became of it I do not know—I don't even have a copy—but as I recall one of its imperatives was temperature. The surface temperature of the water had to rise to 60 degrees before the bass would come into shore, where a boy with no boat could get at them. Until then, they stayed in the deep holes out in the middle, mostly dormant and uninterested in feeding. It seemed an eternity before the water was warm enough. I would pass the same maple tree on the way home from school each day, marking the slow arrival and increase of its green buds as the calendar passed the Ides of March. Indian-summer weather would briefly appear and retreat throughout April in a pattern that kept the water much colder than the air. I carried a thermometer in my pocket and would stop by any streams or ponds I passed to watch for the telltale warming.

As kids, Barry and I had perfected the art of using a flashlight covered with red cellophane to spot the giant nightcrawlers that came out of his yard after a rain. His father was a sportsman who regularly took Barry and his pals fishing and hunting on the Eastern Shore. Perhaps for this reason, his mother was more tolerant of the muss and mud and clutter of boyhood than anyone we knew. She let Barry keep a huge tub full of earth and worms in the basement. It was all the ammunition we needed.

The approach was always the same: a single, barbed 2.0 hook, no leader, tied to 8 lb. test line. We clipped the knot close to the eye of the hook, so as not to give any opportunity for grass to catch on the line and give us away. The worm was impaled in the "collar" and nowhere else, so he could writhe long and well, calling to our prey in the dark and deep. If you had enough line on the reel, the weight of the worm alone would carry a high, long cast to the middle of the pond. The enticing "plip" of the worm on the surface would summon our audience from within

the tree branches. Down, slowly down went the worm. The line steadily sank back toward us until, suddenly, it would shudder to a stop and, after a moment's pause, reverse course, pulled by a swimming bass toward the tree. One, two, three we would count, then pull back for all we were worth, and the fight was on. I watched once as Barry performed this ritual and lifted from the pond a five-pound largemouth bass—the biggest I had ever seen then or since. To this day I have never caught a fish as big, and I hope I never do. The grandest achievements of later life are never so dear as the apogees of our youth.

Time passed, and other springs came and went. I met a girl. I learned to drive. We, who were fools for fishing and truants from our teenage rites of passage, passed through those portals late—but passed them all the same. Barry became a star attackman for our high school lacrosse team and I a midfielder of lesser ability. College, fraternities, parties, marriage, and law school loomed closer then than I knew. My fancy having turned with a vengeance, the assorted packs and traps of my bygone adventures gathered dust in my mother's locker and, eventually, were passed on to those more likely to make use of them. A young man's fancy, indeed. But what of the young man who grows older, still?

As I write this, a poor, misguided robin is spending the day, as he has spent each day for the last seven days, flying a short course from the oak tree that rises in front of our house to the second story window. I await the arrival of spring now from my home in Raleigh, North Carolina, where it comes a little sooner still, but never soon enough. Perhaps I will find my impatience sated one day in Florida, but until then cabin fever will take its yearly toll. Some ornithological strain of the disease surely has dealt a hard blow to the red-breasted dive-bomber who sits outside my window. The little bird's hopeless protest against the transparency of glass is marked by a "tap-tap" of its beak that grows more tedious by the day. This is followed by a flutter of wings as it regains its composure on the windowsill for just a moment before circling off for another sortie against our castle. (What was that song about a billygoat and a hydroelectric dam?)

My wife has become strangely empathetic toward the bird and, with a chauvinism I did not let pass unmentioned, assumed it to be a female looking for a lost chick. She was appropriately outraged when she spied me with our son Kip, one morning, crouched on the sidewalk below the window, planning the bird's assassination with a Daisy BB rifle. After several unsuccessful attempts, at last I had the little pecker in my sights. Then, as I began to squeeze the trigger, I noticed the striking orange of his chest feathers, the "fuller crimson" of which Tennyson wrote, which distinguishes the male of the species. This bird was no anomaly of nature—just another fool for spring, like myself. I lowered the rifle and went inside to finish this essay. Live and let live, I say. It's Spring at last!

The Old Timers, The Old Times

Fall 1995

E very once in a while I catch a whiff of that special
mixture of woodsmoke, coffee, gun-metal and
boot-leather that takes me back there. Way down
in Puryear Hollow, about twelve miles out in the country
beyond Pulaski, Tennessee, lies a shrine of my boyhood
of the kind that too few young people seem to find,
anymore. It was a little house on the farm where my
grandfather was born, planted mostly in tobacco and
beans, with plenty of woods, hills, creeks, and enough
stories for a lifetime. It had wood heat, no indoor
bathroom, no air conditioning, no television, and water
you carried uphill in buckets from a clear, cool spring
when the pump wouldn't prime. In short, it was heaven.
There it was that I came to know my uncles Jefferson
Davis LaCroix and Monroe LaCroix, their sainted wives
Viola and Lucille, and other assorted descendants of the
Frenchmen in my mother's family who first came to farm
and trap those Tennessee foothills two hundred years

earlier. I tagged along for two summers and one deer season as a youngster with Uncle Jeff as he held court under the shade-trees, in the feed-stores, and along the roadsides of Giles County for friends, neighbors, and kids like me. I remember how boys and grown men alike listened to him with the unspoken understanding that here was one of the real "old timers," the genuine article, someone who could talk with authority about the "old days" and who for the most part still lived them.

I got to know Jeff's grown sons Jerry and Charles. Jerry had fun handing me those green, horned tobacco-worms for bream bait and watching for my reaction when he mentioned that they didn't bite "real hard." Charles' dead aim with a gun, the story went, had got him banned from every turkey-shoot in the county. With my own eyes I watched him throw a bright, copper penny up in the air as high as he could, then shoot it out of the sky with a .22 rifle. Incredulous, I retrieved the twisted coin and mailed it back to my brother in Maryland, enclosed with a letter containing a breathless account of this feat. "Could that kill a deer?" I asked Uncle Jeff, as I

admired this amazing weapon in his hands. "Not likely unless you hit him in the head," he replied, "but it will kill you deader than a mackerel." Then he handed me the rifle I would learn to respect, that summer, while plinking tin cans on the hillside.

Those were summers filled with preachin' and sweet harmony on Sundays, hauling hay at three cents a bale, baths in the creek, biscuits for breakfast, Sundrop at lunch, and beans of every species with dinner. Were it not for the considerable time I spent mooning around Farmer Long's pretty daughter up the road, I might never have come out of the woods.

I took away from those summers an understanding of a few of life's rules that have never failed me: That being a lawyer is a whole lot easier than farming; that "Love Lifted (Even) Me"; that there is always room for more chess pie; that farmers' daughters are a fickle breed; and that there is nothing like the great outdoors.

As my son Kip and I glided down the James River in our canoe last weekend, I wondered what he would take with him, and where his shrines will be. These days it seems our approach to the great outdoors has changed from what it was even when I was growing up. We have mostly forgotten the lure of campfires, woodsmoke, black coffee and flapjacks on a camp stove. Today's  adventurer wears neon-fleece outfits and sandals that the old guys wouldn't have been caught dead in; he eats "Power Bars" for lunch, and fishing holes are what he's hell-bent to get through as he races down the river for the maximum adrenaline rush before heading back to the office. Piles of guidebooks written today

will tell you which sections of a river you can run in a day and where to buy a hamburger on your way home, but few will tell you where to pull up and camp. Enter this humble journal.

Let these pages be a guide to the low-tech, high-adventure wilderness experience we need more of. Drop your pack. Pull up your boat. Have a cup of black coffee and a biscuit by the campfire, and watch out for those green, horned worms.

Law and Wilderness

Summary 2002

As I have related in the story about Maine that begins on the next page of this journal, the writings of Henry David Thoreau had an influence on my life that began early and lasted long. He sounded the clarion call to simplicity long before the Kennedys gave us casual chic. Minimalism was his watchword decades before that concept came to symbolize a hip design trend in upscale furniture and art—purchased mostly by people with non-minimalist incomes and lifestyles.

Simplicity and minimalism were for me, in my growing years, mottoes of convenience. It is easy to be simplistic and a minimalist when one hasn't the means to be otherwise. But for all that Thoreau so eloquently tried to tell us about those virtues, I was more struck by Thoreau himself and the ethos of the intellectual rebel that he seemed to embody. His life, more so as I imagined it than likely as he lived it, seemed so defiantly unafraid of convention. And convention, to a teenage boy, is the Lord High Master to be feared and obeyed above all else. To know this we have only to recall our darkest fears of wearing the *wrong* outfit to the dance, getting the *wrong* haircut before going back to school, and saying something stupid in front of the whole class. Thoreau's quiet world on Walden Pond seemed to shrug all of that off, and the notion that someone could live that way—with only his thoughts and principles to condemn or acquit him—was intoxicating to me as I contemplated the power in my hands to shape my own life.

The ability to shape one's life is, of course, the fleeting illusion of youth and the brief luxury of old age. Soon enough we are overtaken by events that shape us and our lives until the mold hardens round about us, immovable and unyielding. The tyranny of the human condition and our need for food, clothing, and comfort lead us onward. Decisions are made. Choices are foregone. Doors close softly behind us. Accidents of geography and genetics work their quiet influence. Soon the trail has narrowed beneath our boots, and before we know it, we can only gaze upon the distant mountains to which other paths less traveled might have led. It was there, on those distant peaks, where Thoreau seemed to stand and beckon to me as an idealistic student reading these words:

Let us consider the way in which we spend our lives. . . .
I foresee that if my wants should be much increased, the
labor required to supply them would become a drudgery.
If I should sell both my forenoons and afternoons to
society, as most appear to do, I am sure that for me there
would be nothing left worth living for. I trust that I
shall never thus sell my birthright for a mess of pottage. I
wish to suggest that a man may be very industrious, and
yet not spend his time well. There is no more fatal
blunderer than he who consumes the greater part of his
life getting his living.

These are lofty ideals, to be sure. What I failed to see as
a younger man, though, was a certain hypocrisy in Thoreau's
words that became clearer to me as a husband and father.
Thoreau's own father had sold pencils from his home to support
young Henry's ascent to Harvard and beyond—and I dare say he
didn't do it for the love of wood and lead. He did it for the love
of Henry, as do we all, in our daily labors, for the love of the
children and families we are privileged to call our burden. Still,
I am not prepared even at this jaded age to toss Thoreau onto
the ash heap of youthful illusions. What Thoreau tried to
express was a sentiment more purely distilled in the famous essay
of his contemporary and fellow-philosopher, Ralph Waldo
Emerson, entitled "Self Reliance":

There is a time in every man's education when he arrives
at the conviction that envy is ignorance; that imitation is
suicide; that he must take himself for better or worse as
his portion; that though the wide universe is full of good,
no kernel of nourishing corn can come to him but
through his toil bestowed on that plot of ground which is
given to him to till. The power which resides in him is
new in nature, and none but he knows what that is
which he can do, nor does he know until he has tried.

As for me, growing up in an alcoholic family on the outskirts of normalcy, the plot of ground I was given to till, as it were, seemed covered in brambles. There was never enough money—or any money. I harbored this deep-seated suspicion that the other guy *really was* smarter than I, and that unlike him, I would become Thoreau's "fatal blunderer," who sells his birthright for a pottage. It was not until I had blundered my way through two colleges, abandoned two majors, and turned four years of undergraduate study into five that the lights went on.

In 1981 I had landed, most improbably, with a wife and a U-Haul van at a Jesuit university in St. Louis to study law. Terrified and broke, I applied myself. Astonished, I succeeded in small ways where I had been accustomed to failure. Encouraged and emboldened, with the support of a wife who loved and believed in me, I applied myself harder still. Doors opened, and the path beneath my boots widened a bit.

That golden moment of epiphany about life's limitless possibilities, which comes to most of us in some form or fashion,

came to me in March 1983. I was approaching the podium of
the law school courtroom. All around me were seated assorted
dignitaries of the bench and bar and academe as well as family
members—including my own mother—who had traveled great
distances to witness the occasion. There were four of us, my
partner Brian Konzen and I and our two opponents, nervously
shuffling papers at the counsel tables. Law school faculty
members whose sandal straps we students were not worthy to
unfasten sat in the audience to witness the spectacle—as if any
of the four of us could possibly have anything important to say
to *them*. I had stolen away, hours before, to a classroom in the
library just to collect my thoughts, alone, and try to bring the
enormity of what I was about to
face down to size. I had never
won anything before. I had
never been in a position to
compete for the prize. Before
this night, dozens of my fellow
students—many from
prominent, successful families
and exclusive, private schools—
had reached for and fallen short
of this goal. Gradually, round
by winning round, I had dispelled my suspicion that we had
survived each preceding contest only by some mistake of good
fortune. I was not even close, after all, to the top of my class.
Were it not for an unexpected friend and unfailing ally I had
encountered along the way, I might have crumpled at the
podium when Justice William Rehnquist of the United States
Supreme Court finally called upon me to deliver the
respondent's argument. That friend and ally is *the law*. It was
then and has been lo these many years a marvel to me, a
fearsome tool, and a thing of beauty in its own right. It is the
great leveler of kings and commoners, and on that night in St.
Louis it elevated a nervous young man from the brambles of his
upbringing to the pinnacle of a legal education.

In the years since, I have taken the memory of our victory in that competition into dozens of other courtrooms, before the mightiest of opponents, before judges who wielded terrible, awesome power. And in each of these arenas, the miracle of our democracy—which is to say the rule of law, not men—has given me the confidence of David before Goliath. This is how I have chosen to spend my life, by and large. Although it has not been the career of contemplative solitude to which Thoreau beckoned me, at Walden Pond, it has had such moments. In fact, I have come to appreciate in my journey through the law that the wilderness is, likewise, a leveler of men.

The wilderness respects no title, fears no enemy, and grants no special privilege. To the unwary or unprepared it is unflinching and unforgiving. It offers no remedy or relief beyond what the laws of nature will allow. But to any mother's son who will apply himself to learn its precepts, great rewards await. You can lose your life in the woods if you are careless, but you can find life's meaning there, too. If you will but study and plan, map your course, and prepare for the journey, you can make your way through any forest of life or nature, no matter what difficulties or delays you have encountered on your journey thus far. Remember to scout the rapids and carry the rough ones. It is best to rise early and find camp before twilight. Gather your firewood before the rain comes, and share it with those who have none. Pitch your tent on high ground, and leave each camp a little better than you found it. These are the laws of the wilderness. These are the laws of life, as well. They are one and the same, and I have been privileged to measure myself against them.

On Simplicity

Winter 2003

Lovers of wilderness paddling and all the wonders it entails—breathtaking scenery, fresh air and solitude being just a few—tend to be lovers of simplicity. Thoreau's exhortation to "simplify, simplify, simplify" might well be the voyageur's credo. After all, we do not take to the woods in buses, but in slender vessels of far more limited capacity. The beauty of a canoe lies not in its versatility but in its singular aptitude to do one thing well and unfailingly, with elegance and grace.

Like many of you, I am one who secretly aspires to a much simpler life. Even so, as I look within a three-foot radius of the computer on which I type the words you now read, I see a veritable storehouse of supplies inessential to life on Earth. There are assorted brass curios, pens that long since went dry, books I will never read, copies of useless documents, and file cabinets to keep it all in pointless order. In the rooms beyond my office, the stockpile of life's miscellany expands farther still.

Perhaps it is the clutter and complexity of civilized life that compels us to the woods. Set his feet in a canoe, and even the most prodigious packrat among us must be content with a mere ration of the impedimenta considered "essential" to life at home. When I empty the contents of my pack in search of some item at the bottom, often I will pause to marvel at how Spartan are the tools of the outdoor life. With one eye to the portage that lies ahead, I cast the other critically upon any goods which might have been weeded out, vowing next time to be more vigilant against such needless excess. When we are in the woods for more than a few days' duration, we eat less and more simply, and what we have in abundance are not possessions, but our thoughts—and the time to think them.

My fascination with the ideal of simplicity began early, though it would lie fallow for many years thereafter. It was 1964, at the World's Fair. New York seemed to me, as a six-year-old, an exceedingly long distance from my home in Baltimore, though probably it was not much more than a three-hour drive. I don't recall being a party to any lengthy preparations to go (I usually was not consulted in advance about such matters), only that it was dark and traffic was busy on St. Paul Street when I suddenly found myself in the back of the family car at what ordinarily would have been way past my bedtime.

The World's Fair itself is mostly a blur in my memory. I have a vague recollection of people in strange, African dress beating out a rhythm on bongo drums of some kind—pretty exotic stuff for a little boy from Baltimore. I also recall the giant, steel globe of planet Earth, placed prominently on the grounds, that was the most visible symbol of something momentous and important going on. Something momentous and important, indeed. Yes, I understood even then that it was not an everyday sort of thing to go to a World's Fair. It was a wonderland, for sure—a bazaar filled with intricate, native crafts of every description. Yet for me, the most enduring memory of the trip is what little I brought home. Of all the trinkets and souvenirs that the world had laid before me at the fair, I chose nothing more than one carved, wooden donkey from some pueblo in South America. It was smaller than the palm of my hand.

I recall thinking how pitiful it was that a child should return from so grand an adventure with so meager a trophy. I also distinctly remember knowing, at the time, that my self-pity was contrived. My mother and sisters had asked me more than once whether that was all I really wanted. Determined to play St. Francis, I reveled in my self-imposed deprivation. No grasping, gluttonous striver, I—no sir! I would learn to be content in my want, however imaginary it might be.

All false piety aside, there is, undeniably, a quiet power that resides in poverty. Part of that power is drawn from the virtue of a simple life. What we don't have cannot be taken from us, and what cannot be taken from us we need not fear having to do without. This was the wisdom of Rabbi Schachtel, now also the words of a pop song: "Happiness is not having what you want, but wanting what you have."

A sailor and favorite author of mine, Don Casey, tells a story of the first Dole plantation in the South Pacific: "None of the islanders came back to work after the first two weeks, having earned enough money in their first paycheck to buy everything for sale in the stores of their village." Casey wryly observes that if there had been a Wal-Mart on the island, many of them would be working, still. Perhaps that is the story of our island.

The bedrock of the American economy is freedom, growth, and prosperity—freedom to pursue a prosperity measured by growth in the number and value of our possessions. The lifestyle we encounter in the wilderness is the antithesis of this principle. In place of "things," we find a seamless harmony of life, death, and regeneration. The qualities we seek in the

wilderness have nothing to do with the number or value of the possessions we take with us, there. "Growth" in the wild takes on a new meaning. The forest is always growing, but left unattended a mature wilderness will appear very much the same in a hundred years as it does today. How does your neighborhood look, compared to a hundred years ago? In place of luxuries, afield, we carry tools, implements, and vessels of practical and necessary use. Typically, the inventory of equipment one brings to the woods will shrink—not grow— with time and experience. Look around your house: is there more or less stored there, today, than a decade ago?

How do we reconcile the complexity of our civilized world with the simplicity of the wilderness that we so admire and love? There was a time when I would have met that dichotomy with the youthful zeal of absolutism—with exhortations to sell up, pare down, cut back, and go native. But I have grown more skeptical, in my forty-five years, of the absolutist. Life's answers rarely are so obvious.

Consider our friend, Mr. Thoreau. More than merely an apostle of simplicity and leisure, he stood atop the shoulders of a prosperous, young nation to condemn the very industry that bore him to those heights. Were it not for the hard labor of nameless cobblers, farmers, miners and sailors—and the bloody shores of Bunker Hill where they died—Thoreau's neck might have been beneath the boot of a British soldier instead of craning to hear the call of the whippoorwill on the Allagash. He traveled to the North Woods on wheels of iron, dug from the earth by men who scarcely knew a summer's day of ease, and tempered by fire in the choking smoke of Pennsylvania foundries—a far cry from the tufted parlors of Concord and Cambridge. Many of us are no different than he.

Statistically speaking, that some of us even live, today, is a study in complexity of the highest order. Who discovered the vaccines that saved you from polio and smallpox and measles? Who built the laboratories in which they were conceived? Who mined the sand which became the glass which became the test tubes in which these miracles took shape? Who built the machines by which these materials were mined, or the roads over which they came to market? What of the workers who made all of this happen? Do we suppose that they were paid in platitudes and psalms? Was it not money they sought—money to buy comfort and ease and vaccines for their own children; money which paid the salary of the brilliant scientist, who paid his carpenter, who built his lovely home, who by his wages sent his own child to college, and who by that child's industry added to the body of science and, in turn, to our abundance?

Most of us well know the parable of the rich young man, who refused to sell all his worldly goods and give the proceeds to the poor. Some mistake this story as a call to universal poverty, but implicit in Christ's instruction to the rich man is the necessity of a willing buyer. Unless we suppose that Christ intended the rich man's obedience to be the occasion of another man's sin, we must conclude that it is not in owning things that we falter, but in things owning us. Real virtue lies in our state of mind, not in the quantity of our goods, however many or few. It takes a simple man to know the difference.

Time, Speed & Distance

Spring 1996

Dressed in battle gear of Bean Boots and old chinos, I sat perched behind the window of my office. A gray, winter sky loomed above downtown New Bern. A Jeep in the parking lot below waited at the ready, fully packed for a weekend on the Cape Fear River. But as I looked across town, a freezing downpour continued to tap out a steady reminder of the impudence of nature. The Cape Fear is new water to me, and the guides warn of "an absolute keeper hydraulic" in periods of high water (read: a big nasty spot in the water offering a one-way swimming invitation). Class II rapids are reported along the route, flooding to Class III with rain.

Having long since put my young son's outfit back in the shed, promising him later adventures in calmer, warmer waters, I was still loathe to surrender the two free days set aside for this trip. I had lifted the canoe onto

the Jeep under a clear, moonlit sky the night before, but the rain thudding on the roof by dawn told the tale. Maybe it would clear, I thought. Then again, the neighbors would think I'd finally lost my mind if I drove through our little town in that weather with a canoe on top of the car. "Was that Mike Hurley I saw headed off in a freezing gale with a canoe?" I carried it back to the shed.

My computer's cursor blinked at me impatiently, and I glanced out the window for any break in the clouds. The rain came harder, with more purpose. It is Springtime in the South. Tulips and azaleas must be given their due, and fair weather waits for no man. Thus are we all reminded that the pace of nature is not the pace of clocks and deadlines, weekends and holidays. For most of man's days on this earth he has kept in rhythm with the natural cycles of time. Life's routine was clearly divided by light and dark, warm and cold, wind and calm. Ours is now a world that heats and cools our air to order, lights our malls all night long, and moves us about in aerodynamic bullets along smooth, paved roads.   Into this even order comes the effrontery of rain clouds, hurricanes and blizzards, running through precious free-space on the calendar while we can only wait.

It rained a little harder still.   I stayed inside. Bean Boots soon grow hot, indoors. There would be no trip today.

It was another rainy morning in September 1994 when I eased the bow of an old fishing canoe over the lawn of the town pond in Old Forge, New York. Two hundred fifty paddlers, myself among them, awaited the start of the Adirondack Canoe Classic—a 90-mile, three-day dash across the ancient "highway" of the fur traders and Indians. We all clung to coffee cups and shuffled our feet to stave off the morning chill. The weekend after Labor Day had brought Fall to this country as surely as the mail.

As my eighty-pound, fifteen-foot, tandem canoe readily attested, I was not hoping to win—only to finish. A veteran of the event passing by stopped to ask, "Are you planning to race in that thing?" I said I was. He asked to shake my hand with that admiration usually accorded to condemned men, and I began to feel the unease of one realizing he arrived an hour ago at the wrong party. Try as I might, it was hard to appear nonchalant paddling a tandem fishing-boat in a racing event, with a full pack lodged in the bow for weight.

It wasn't that bad, really. In fact I rather enjoyed the challenge of paddling that old barge for three days from Old Forge to Saranac Lake. It was one of the few times that I had ever paddled with a sense of real purpose to get somewhere across a span of time and distance. As brisk, blue skies broke through and the sun rose over the water, it was a great day to be alive and straining behind the ash. Yet unlike the average day of canoeing spent idling for fish and pleasure, the limitations of a paddle applied at a given speed over a span of time and distance are immutable in a race. Stroke, glide, correct, stroke . . . The end of a lake miles away comes only so slowly closer. On this highway of the Adirondacks, there was no accelerator, no cruise control, no amount of hurrying to propel the trappers and the Mohawk toward their goals. Nothing but the unerring addition of stroke to stroke.

The raw boundaries of the natural world and the limits of traversing it under one's own power are no more in evidence than on a portage. A particularly brutal one of nearly two miles around Raquette Falls, mostly up the side of a mountain, waited for us on the second day. Years ago I had often pursued the limits of my physical endurance on the lacrosse field, but I believe I found those limits at last on the Raquette Falls portage beneath an eighty-pound canoe. It seemed as though it would never end, but each time I dropped the weight from my aching shoulders, subconsciously seeking to plead some compromise of

the situation, none was granted. A distance remained to be covered, and only the application of time to speed would span it.

Ultimately, the simple propulsion of paddle and muscle over time and distance fetched Saranac Lake with a seeming swiftness, in hindsight, that was not discernible in the medium of the moment. My mother often remarks when she looks at my wisp of a daughter that she remembers herself as just such a little girl "like it was yesterday." The same laws of memory must be at work in the paddle.

It is still raining outside, but in my mind's eye I remember the glint of the water at the end of the portage below Raquette Falls. I'm content to wait. The time and distance from rain to sunshine, from winter to summer, from youth to old age, are just so many paddle strokes subtracted from the number God has given us. We all get there eventually. What's our hurry, anyway?

The Gypsy in Me

Spring 2003

I n the eulogy to my father, which I struggled to read
through an unexpected wave of emotion eleven years
ago at Arlington, I felt compelled to remind myself
and my siblings that "[s]ooner or later, . . . we have to
come to terms with our roots. We did not invent
ourselves. We are the sons and daughters of our parents.
And if today my brother and sisters and I dream great
dreams and seek the adventure in life with a childlike
faith in the future, we would be only fooling ourselves
not to acknowledge the dreamer and adventurer who has
gone before us, the tragedy of whose alcoholism stood
between him and his dreams." A year ago this May, with
the passing of our mother, I had occasion to contemplate
these words anew.

All of us struggle, at this milestone, to gain some
perspective on that chapter of life which is our own
childhood—a chapter whose last enduring symbol

vanishes with the death of our parents. The memories of those days lie scattered on the floor awhile, as we search for a theorem of remembrance—a box of sorts, constructed of the questions and answers that will both contain and explain our past. Not until these images are given order and meaning can they be safely stored in the closets of our minds, where we are free to return from time to time in search of answers to the questions in life that lie ahead.

Like many of her generation, my mother was not a coddler or a nervous hen. By necessity more than design, she gave me—a latchkey kid from a young age—a degree of personal freedom that I found absolutely delicious. The world really was my oyster. Each sunny afternoon and every creek and wood-lot beckoned me with undetermined potential. I can't help but notice the evolution in parenting styles since those years. Child psychologist John Redmond describes the change this way: Whereas children once revolved in orbit around their parents' lives and thus learned the crucial lesson that they are not the center of the universe, parents' lives today revolve in orbit around their children, who not surprisingly have an inflated sense of their own importance. At a school athletic-awards banquet I recently attended, there was more effusive praise for the talent of sixth-grade outfielders than I suspect Willie Mays heard during his induction into the Hall of Fame.

Parents in the 60's, my mother included, worked all week and looked forward to a little R&R for themselves on the weekend. As kids we pretty much did our own thing. Sometimes we got gloriously into trouble, but we acquired a sense of adventure and a capacity to dream that children now, in their over-scheduled, over-supervised lives, have been denied. Tell a ten-year old child of today's soccer moms just to "go out and play," and you might very well get a blank stare.

Looking back at that first eulogy from the distance of eleven years, the image of the dreamer and adventurer in both of my parents remains bright. That, I suppose, is their legacy to me. For my father, the product of a privileged upbringing and an ivy league education, alcoholism barred the way to any lasting accomplishment in life. Still, he retained an indefatigable and, at times, infuriating optimism—optimism that he would strike gold in the Rockies, finally develop a system for picking ponies at the track, or make it big, overnight, in business. He was no model father, by any means, yet I cannot help but smile when I think of him celebrating his move to Mazatlan, in his late seventies, to the tune of "Who needs you, I've got Mexico." If I hit rock bottom someday and need to reach for that kind of chutzpah to pull myself up, I hope I find it as readily as he did.

For my mother, herself the child of an alcoholic, her gender and the tenor of her times, the unexpected birth of the youngest son of a failed marriage, and a limited education should have defeated her, but she succeeded remarkably in spite of these obstacles. She worked two jobs, leaving me and the family dog alone in our apartment to a world of late-night Elvis movies and frozen TV dinners. She found a niche in federal civil service, moved us to the suburbs, and made a fatherless childhood as close to normal as she reasonably could accomplish, given our circumstances. Through it all, she kindled a wild and almost tragically comic desire for wealth and notoriety, just as she remained commitedly skeptical of our well-to-do neighbors and the veneer of normalcy that distinguished their lives from ours.

One of the second jobs my mother held to make ends meet was a position in the admitting office of Johns Hopkins University Hospital, where I had been born in 1958. Diaper service for her new son was a luxury beyond her means, but not her imagination. She offered to slip the driver of the diaper truck the names of new mothers coming home from the hospital. The diaper service gained an uncanny intuition for finding new customers, and I got all the free, clean diapers I needed. It was part of a pattern of benign subterfuge that, I would later come to recognize, marked her approach to many things in life. She was a Gypsy at heart, just like the Irishman she married. If she dreamed of wealth and comfort, it was only to be a wealthier and more comfortable Gypsy—never a matron of the stuffy, polite society she loathed. This definition of her nature eluded me until, earlier this spring, I recalled the story she often told of her encounter with a kindred spirit—the Gypsy Queen.

She was an ancient woman of Eastern European heritage who arrived at Johns Hopkins Hospital with an entourage. It fell to my mother, as the admissions officer, to gather all the particulars. When she asked for the woman's age, however, her co-workers gasped and summoned her out of earshot of the waiting family. "Do you know who that is?" they whispered. "She's the queen of the Gypsies! You don't ask them for her age! She has no age. They believe she is immortal." Composing herself, my mother returned to her desk and proceeded with the interview—omitting any further references to age.

As word spread that the Gypsy Queen was a patient at the hospital, telegrams began arriving from around the world, as did throngs of well wishers and van loads of flowers. Days passed, and the outlook became increasingly grim. Then came the news that she had passed away. One caller demanded to know the name of her attending physician, which my mother obligingly provided. Minutes later, the physician appeared at the window of the admitting office, ashen faced. "Don't tell anyone I was her doctor," he begged. "Why ever not?" my mother asked, still not fully aware of the stature of this patient. "Because immortals are not supposed to die."

The hospital waiting room soon was filled with a cacophony of mourners who arrived by droves from New York in long, black Cadillacs. The attending physicians snuck out through the back entrance to avoid them. The Gypsy Queen was no more, or so it seemed.

In 1976 I left our two-bedroom apartment on a bus for college, the last of four children and the youngest by ten years. For the first time, at age 55, my mother was on her own. She wasted no time. She bought a new car, moved to a rented house in a tony suburb on the outskirts of Washington, D.C., and began a long-awaited adventure in independence. She traveled widely in her work for the government, visiting elderly shut-ins in little country towns to help them qualify for social security benefits. It was a Gypsy life, and she loved every minute of it. She often supplemented her expense account to gain a taste of the good stuff at fancy restaurants and stay at finer hotels. After I got a job, I would try to impress her with expensive dinners. "I've had better," she would quip. My mother was always a little rough around the edges, a little insecure—even rude at times— but her message rang true: Live life to the hilt, and don't be fooled by appearances.

Eight months after my mother's death, my twelve-year old son and I stood on a dock in Charleston contemplating the purchase of "Moonlighter," a 32-foot sailboat built in 1979 that I hoped would take us on our own Gypsy adventures, someday. She was a little rough around the edges and lacked the finer appointments of a proper yacht, but she seemed sound. The surveyor said her hull was "as hard as a New York sidewalk," but the clincher was on the abstract of title: The original owner had named her "The Gypsy In Me." In a nod to seagoing superstition against re-naming boats, I took part of each name and christened her the "Gypsy Moon." Friends and I sailed her offshore to North Carolina over three cloudless days and two moonlit nights. Along the way I drank a toast to the Gypsy in me, and to the mother of adventure in all of us. Long may she live.

A Boy's Life

Summer 2003

What a remarkable voyage it has been. My son Kip turned thirteen in June of this year. As we paddled together in August—just the two of us—for eight days and seven nights through that holy wilderness of Northern Minnesota, I scarcely recognized the powerful figure in the bow of the canoe. There, where for years had sat a little tow-headed boy playing with frogs and bugs and hardly ever noticing a paddle, was a solid, young man matching me stroke for stroke. It has been a change long in coming but so quick in its passing that, lately, I have felt the urge to rub my eyes in disbelief. My elders used to preface their observations of me with the words "it was only yesterday," and now I know the derivation of that phrase.

   We have been through countless adventures afloat, the two of us. On innumerable lakes, rivers, and two oceans, through capsizings and storms, suffering rains that lasted for weeks and reveling beneath eternal, sunny skies, Kip has been my most faithful companion. We don't choose our fathers, but the choice made for us holds the potential to color all that we do and are. A fisherman's son will learn to fish, and a sailor's son to ply the wind. He may travel on to other skills and interests, but the avocations of his youth will always bear a fond familiarity. Like a first instrument in the hands of its former student, the memories of those days will play sweeter still in the distant years of old age.

Many readers who love the voyageur's life as I do would suppose that Kip Hurley is living a charmed youth, but to Kip it is the only life he has known—no more or less charming than any other he might imagine. Watching the moon rise over a dot of water in a distant forest; savoring the taste of a fish grilled only moments after it was caught; listening to stories beside a crackling campfire in a home built of canvas and canoe paddles; drifting off to sleep, night after night, to the peaceful serenade of running water—these glories have simply been part of the wallpaper of his boyhood. He has splashed and played in a hundred waterfalls more spectacular than any theme park, but like every child he pines for the day his parents will take him to ride the log flume at Disney World. I jokingly tell him and his

sister that they've been
living in Disney World all
these years without
knowing it, and they
groan.

Through it all I
have been cognizant of
Kip's silent and oblique
observation of my habits,
the way a cottontail rabbit
sees our approach without
turning its head to look.
I have worn uncom-
fortably the mantle of
fatherhood, ever doubtful of God's decision to cast me in the
role of leading man in the drama of a child's life. There are,
after all, no dress rehearsals, and the critics can be brutal.

It occurred to me, as we wound our way through the
spectacular scenery of the Boundary Waters, this summer, that
Kip's adolescence would be not only his right of passage, but
mine, as well. I had been called to be a beacon and a guide to
this child before I had yet escaped the fog of my own boyhood,
and it would be my challenge to steer us both clear without
running up on the rocks. Unanswerable questions disturb my
peace of mind: Will there be problems with drugs or alcohol?
Will he talk to me? Will I find the words to help? Will my own
example inspire or discourage him? Will he choose wisely? Will
he find good friends to ground him? In moments of doubt, will
he find faith?

I am mindful that questions such as these are no less
pertinent to that tousle of blonde hair, freckles and elbows that is
my eleven-year-old daughter, Caroline. Nor do I suppose that
the kindly offices of a father extend only to a son's coming of

age. Caroline is the patient student of all that I attempt to teach her, but for now at least, the storms in her life are mostly those peculiar to the lives of little girls. In such matters her mother offers a steadier hand on the tiller. I suffer the disadvantage of inexperience. What I happily give her is a willing ear, a hand to hold, and a welcome shoulder. What she will take from me, ultimately, is nothing less than the standard by which, for good or ill, she will measure every other man she encounters in life. Whether in the end I rise to that challenge or falter beneath it is not my essay to write.

The eternal question that confounds fathers and sons is simply this: What does it mean to be a good man? The lives of great men in history offer us examples to follow, of course, but the devil lives in the interpretation of example. One might suppose that at least the outer markers of right and wrong are visible to all, but I grow less certain of that with time.

A few months ago I was on my way to work when the driver of a shiny, black BMW to my left on a two-lane road veered suddenly toward me. Inches away from his passenger door, I jammed my brakes hard and steered to the right.

I avoided what would have been a bad wreck for both of us, but
the right wheels on my car were bent when I hit the curb. The
driver of the BMW stopped and accepted responsibility for the
damage. Dressed in a suit and presenting a business card that
revealed him to be a high-ranking bureaucrat in state
government, he implored me to replace my battered wheels and
send the bill directly to him—asking that I not involve his
insurance company. I thankfully agreed, and we shook hands.
After I replaced the wheels and sent him the bill a few days later,
I received a reply from his attorney, denying responsibility for

the accident. With no police report and no witnesses, I realized I had foolishly trusted in the value of something I assumed to be priceless: a man's word, sealed by a handshake.

Examples of this sort of deceit and far worse are hardly newsworthy, but it is always startling to encounter it in one's own affairs, behind a smiling face. Kip, who lovingly guards my car out of longing for the day he will be allowed to drive it, was incensed by the man's deception. The whole experience was little more than an annoyance, but it taught us a valuable lesson. We were reminded that every man must choose to put personal responsibility ahead of personal advantage. Although I am ill-qualified to make pious claims of selfless virtue, I can say with confidence that Kip has learned never to shake a man's hand with the intention to deceive him. That particular shoal in life, for now, should be plainly in view. Others will be less easily spotted. My sobering duty as his father will be to guide him chiefly by example. In this daunting task, I solicit your prayers.

As Kip and I headed out from Thomas Lake last August, on the morning of our sixth day in the Boundary Waters, we celebrated our uncommon, good fortune. The weather and the fishing could not have been better. Well rested and refreshed, we boldly decided to paddle all the way to Disappointment Lake, that day, and set up camp for two nights. Moving westward, however, we began to encounter other parties of canoes, and it became clear that there would be fierce competition for campsites at the end of the day. We resolved to stop before reaching Disappointment and take the next campsite we saw, possibly on Ahsub Lake.

As we paddled on I noticed an older man from Iowa. Traveling with his grandchildren, he had given us a wide smile when we first saw him, earlier in the week. On this day he was having trouble staying ahead of Kip and me. Catching his breath at the end of one portage, he struck up a conversation

and asked where we intended to camp. I told him that Ahsub Lake was a possibility. He took out a rumpled map that looked like it might have made this trip twenty years ago, and pointed to one of only two sites on Ahsub Lake. "That's where we'd like to camp," he said. His boys looked worn out. I knew we could beat them there and that the old man was asking me, as best his pride would let him, to pass up that site. I assured him we were going much farther, that day.

When Kip and I arrived that afternoon at the head of the last portage, we were spent. Three couples sat at the waters' edge, watching us as we came ashore. They told us they were camped nearby and felt sure that all the sites on Disappointment Lake were taken. "Hence, the name," I said. They laughed. One of them complimented Kip on the broken fishing pole we had splinted together with sticks and duct tape. He squirmed at the attention and hurried down the trail. I followed with our canoe on my shoulders. As we paused at the other end to make a plan for that night, we heard something behind us. There, coming across the portage on the shoulders of the couples we had just met, were the rest of our heavy packs. It was a welcome reprieve. Not long thereafter, we found the best campsite of the trip. Things often seem to work out that way. My hope is that the years ahead offer Kip many such reasons to recall that a good man seeks something higher than his own advantage, and that a good life is its own reward.

The View from Here

Fall 2003

I t has been more than eight years since that summer in 1995 when, camped alone under a full moon on the shores of Long Pond, in the St. Regis area of the Adirondacks, I got the wild hare to write and publish a canoeing journal. I was euphoric finally to be doing at age 37 what I had only imagined as a boy, and I wanted to tell the world. I hoped to create something that would serve not merely to chronicle my personal adventures but to sing the glories of wilderness voyaging. It was apparent to me that the romance of travel by paddle and portage had somehow been lost on the over-engineered, hyper-technical camper of today, whose chief aim, it seemed, was to put as many layers of Gore-Tex as possible between himself and an authentic, wilderness experience. I wanted to restore through the olfactory of language that whiff of woodsmoke, balsam, hot coffee, and bacon frying on an open fire that was all but unknown to a new generation of shopping-mall adventurers.

This lark on the banks of Long Pond was not the first time I had indulged delusions of journalistic grandeur. There had been flashes in the pan, before: various impromptu college newspapers, occasional magazine articles, and a forged press-pass that let me inside the police line at the ERA rally in Washington, where I got to shoot pictures of Marlo Thomas eating an apple and gaze in amazement at Bella Abzug's enormous hat. There were daydreams, when I should have been studying for finals, about launching this or that magazine. The bug to write for public consumption had bitten me early in life, and recovery from infections of this sort is usually hopeless.

Mine was an unusual strain of the writer's virus which compelled me to instruct readers in a subject as a means of coming to understand it for the first time, myself. Thus did I find the chutzpah to write, at the grizzled age of thirteen, a pamphlet telling others how to improve their bass fishing when I had scarcely caught a dozen, respectable fish on my own. The journal you now read was cut from the same cloth. Someone once said, "Act like you know what you're doing, and the world is your oyster." I can think of no better credo for trial lawyers, politicians, and outdoor adventure writers.

The truth is that I knew precious little about canoe camping when I set out to publish a quarterly journal on the subject, and I still know less than most of you. Although I paddled occasionally as a boy scout on camping trips, canoe travel in the tradition of North Woods voyageurs was something beyond my understanding.

An opportunity arose one year to join other scouts on a much-ballyhooed trip to the Boundary Waters Canoe Area Wilderness in Minnesota, but lack of money to travel such a long distance (well before the days of discount airfares) kept me and many others at home. Sitting with my fellow wallflowers in the dark, on the dusty, wood floor of the church hall where the scout troop spent Friday nights, I watched as a clackety projector produced a flickering, black-and-white movie of two boys canoeing through Canada. They carried their gear in great, canvas packs and dined off of their talents at the rod and reel. Seeing this mode of travel for the first time, I was transported. I dreamt of the day I would experience similar adventures on my own.

The dreams of one's early boyhood fade quickly, alas. I became an athlete and an inveterate Romeo in high school and college. This transformation was followed rapidly by other, head-snapping bends in the road: marriage at 23, law school immediately thereafter, and then a career as an associate in a big law firm. I was nearly 30 before I took my first day of vacation. It was not until after I had a son of my own and he turned four that my old dream of a loaded canoe, a placid lake, and a waiting wilderness came rushing back like a torrent.

I was in Rocky Mount, North Carolina, at the time, at a discount warehouse store. My wife casually pointed out a 15-foot, red Coleman canoe hanging from the rafters. I should have suspected that there was some voodoo afoot when she did this. After all, she is the non-sailor who casually mentioned, one day in Houston, that we might visit the sailboat store behind our tiny apartment. The thought of buying a sailboat had never occurred to me. Four years and two boats later, we still had not bought a house. Four years after that, we sold our first house and moved to the coast of North Carolina so that I could chase the life of a professional sea captain.

It was the first canoe I had ever seen for sale in a store. In the places I had lived—Maryland, Missouri, Texas, and North Carolina, in that order—there were row boats and rafts aplenty on display at sporting goods outlets, but never a canoe. That day in Rocky Mount, where others saw merely another boat, I saw a $350 magic carpet—a lifetime-pass to all of the wilderness adventures I had imagined as a child. People in the store were walking right by it, oblivious to its beguiling invitation, but it called to me like a genie in a bottle. I bought it, of course. Had I not, this might have been a journal about stamp collecting, instead.

A 15-foot, polyethylene-over-aluminum frame "Ram-X" is hardly the stuff of legend. Sigurd Olson and Bill Mason did not wax sentimental over the good ol' Coleman canoe. It is, nonetheless, the preferred battle-wagon of Southern float-fishermen everywhere—those determined fellows, fueled by little cans of Vienna sausages and beans, who will beat any boat to within a skinny inch of its life in pursuit of stringers of bass and bream. If there is poetry in such a vessel, it is a short work.

Before long, though, I was experimenting with various ideas for making a silk purse out of a sow's ear, and a wilderness-tripping canoe out of my investment.

I tried all kinds of gear and packing strategies, including portage wheels, cargo nets, and five-gallon ice-cream buckets with water-tight lids. After awhile, I discovered that there usually is more science than sentiment in traditional ways of doing things. The reason the canvas Duluth pack, portage yoke, and campfire tent have been around for more than a century is that they all do a simple job well. And however much we improve and innovate modern methods and materials, there will never be a vessel made of plastic that dips and sways so sweetly, or rests so beautifully in the eye of the beholder, as a wooden canoe. This journal became a compendium of such lessons as I learned them, and a celebration of traditions that have stood the test of time.

But I digress. I did not begin this final essay to write the last 34 essays over again. If you have been with me for the journey, you know these stories, and I hope they have brought a smile or two. What perhaps you don't know, and what I am coming to learn only lately myself, is the driving force behind them.

The journal has for me been the literary equivalent of two soup cans strung together between twenty yards of cord. The excitement at seeing a personal daydream come to fruition, in print, is something akin to hearing your pal's voice echo on the other end of that cord, even though he's standing in a treehouse close enough to shout the message to you just as clearly. I could have written these stories and essays for any number of canoeing publications and perhaps made a larger reputation for myself—not to mention more money—but they would not have held the same thrill for the writer. A child could more efficiently navigate a river in a store-bought skiff than to spend the better part of an afternoon lashing together logs, but he would not as easily conjure the spirit of Huckleberry Finn.

At the heart of every pamphleteer and kitchen-table publisher, whose exemplar is Benjamin Franklin, is a yearning to do something large in a small and unexpected way. Therein lies the reason this journal bears more in common with Poor Richard's Almanac than the typical, Hook 'em and Cook 'em outdoor-magazine of today's Madison Avenue publishers. Nothing in all of the outdoors more readily deflates my spirit than a fast, shiny boat, bristling with horsepower and electronics, varooming off in pursuit of some testosterone-charged ideal of a wilderness experience. I would rather command the helm of a single clipper ship in a modern-day reprise of the East Indian spice-trade than a fleet of luxury ocean-liners. A penchant for the unlikely conquest, for self-expression unbounded by convention, is what has driven me to write—and I dare say what compels you to read—this pamphlet of mine. What I have been attempting, almost unawares, to express on these pages is an argument for choosing the path less traveled. I have trod upon, turned from, and regained that path dozens of times, myself. Every word I have written has been taken from the same, unfinished essay that I now see, looking back from the perspective of these past eight years, I have been writing all my life.

Long-time readers of this journal will know the story of my decision at age 30 to leave a comfortable existence on the partnership track of a law firm in Houston to begin, without a single client or a single case, a firm of my own in 1988. It was not an entirely new idea. I had stumbled upon and quickly devoured a book in law school entitled *How to Go Directly Into Solo Practice Without Missing A Meal.* Only through the gentle persuasion of my ethics professor, Dennis Tuchler, had I forgone the idea of starting my own practice right after graduation. "Are you worried I won't have any clients?" I asked. "No," he said. "I'm worried you'll have too many." I recall to this day the kindness of his concern as much as the enormity of his intellect.

After four years at Hays, McConn, Rice and Pickering, with a half-dozen jury trials under my belt and an over-inflated opinion of my abilities, I left to open the law offices of Michael C. Hurley. At an open house for my new office, pals from my old firm gave me a gift that well expressed the inauspiciousness of the moment: a plaque reading, "Cash only—no checks, please." The ripple effect of that decision to strike out on my own, however, still astonishes me, and in the process I learned that America is yet a Land of Opportunity for all. Within three years we had become the husband and wife firm of Hurley & Hurley, employing six attorneys and as many staff, and ranked 41st on the "Houston 100" list of the fastest growing businesses in the fourth largest city in the nation. We moved into new offices in a gleaming, glass tower on the fashionable side of town, with hardwood floors, oriental rugs, and spacious views of the Texas plain to the west. One of the old-line firms in town offered us a handsome partnership to subsume our practice into its own, and we turned them down flat. Our collections approached a million dollars a year. I was no wealthier than most of my peers, but I was at one of the higher ledges near the top of Unlikely Mountain, and the sky was the limit. No sooner had the paint dried on the walls of our new office, however, when a feeling of unease overtook me—a clutch in my gut that made me wonder if I really wanted to be where I was at the time, and what I might rather be doing with the rest of my life.

Julie planned to leave the firm indefinitely with the birth of our second child, but that alone was not reason enough for me to sell our practice, fold up our tent, and move away to become a sailboat charter captain in a tiny town on the coast of North Carolina. At the time I could have given you any number of reasons why I decided to leave, including the honest

desire to spend more time with the fascinating little human beings our children were becoming. Such a cataclysmic change, though, would hardly be necessary to achieve those aims. Looking back at those days, now, I have to wonder if the force at work was not an abiding distrust of power, privilege, largesse, and conformity. Some might call it a fear of success or a low threshold for boredom, but I would disagree. It is the same force that has propelled this improbable publication to kick against the goad of convention. Who, after all, would suppose that anyone cared to read a homespun, black-and-white, low-budget journal on canoe-camping in this age of glossy, color magazines and high-tech extreme sports? More than ten thousand of you, in fact, cared enough to subscribe, and I have been more flattered than you know to be your poet and guide.

My Bohemian impulses have been constrained for a little while by the loving necessity to provide bed and board for two special children, but time marches on. Out there, somewhere, I can hear the faint, distant beat of a different drummer. I am headed his way. Keep a lamp lit for me, my friends, and for the adventures in life that still await us all.

Index of Photographs

Notes: *All photographs are by Michael C. Hurley unless otherwise attributed. The season and year in each photo caption refers to the date the photograph was taken, not the issue of the journal in which it appeared.*

Page   Caption

xii   High Falls on the Oswegatchie River in the Adirondacks, Spring 1997.

xv   Author unloads a canoe at camp on Attean Pond in Maine, Summer 1998.

xvi   Kip Hurley searches for skipping rocks on the Potomac River, Summer 1997.

2   Eastern painted turtle on the Batsto River in the New Jersey Pine Barrens, Fall 1998.

3   Kip Hurley runs up the side of an island in La Verendrye Reserve in Quebec, Summer 1999.

4   End of the portage in the Boundary Waters Canoe Area Wilderness, Summer 2003.

8   Kip Hurley waits for a dinner of steamed, freshly caught mussels on Diamond Lake in Temagami Canoe Country, Ontario, Summer 2000.

11   Caroline Avery, with Claire Shields in the background, rides an impromptu rope-swing hung from a tree by our campsite along the Tyger River in South Carolina, Summer 1998.

14   Terry and Becky Rich paddle at dawn on Crooked Lake in the Boundary Waters Canoe Area Wilderness, Summer 1996.

15   Overlooking the Oswegatchie River, several miles below High Falls and above Cranberry Lake in the Adirondacks, Spring 1997.

16   Author's canoe pointed upstream from a landing on the Delaware River, Spring 2000.

221

Page *Caption*

21   Author overlooking Lac La Perche in La Verendrye Reserve, Quebec, Summer 1999. Photo by Michael Rosenthal.

22   From left to right: Author, Kip Hurley, Bennett Rosenthal, Michael Rosenthal, and Robin Lauer in camp on Lac La Perche in La Verendrye Reserve, Quebec, Summer 1999.

24   Michael Rosenthal paddles son Bennett and Kip Hurley on the last leg of a trip in La Verendrye Reserve, Quebec, Summer 1999.

26   The author's uncle, Ted Hurley, and family friend on Long Island Sound, circa. 1950. Ted is at the helm of his 42-foot auxiliary sailing cutter, *Cygnet*, formerly the *Florence*, designed and built by James E. Graves Shipyard of Marblehead, Massachusetts in 1916.

27   View of the Moose River in Maine, from the location of an abandoned cabin above Holeb Falls, Summer 1998.

28   Native brook trout taken by the author on the first ledge at Camel Rips on the Moose River in Maine, Summer 1998. Also shown are "short ribs" in author's canoe.

32   Author and wife Julie, leaving Our Lady of the Fields Catholic Church, in Millersville, Maryland, on their wedding day in 1981.

34   Looking south toward the Beartrap River from the head of the portage to Iron Lake, in the Boundary Waters Canoe Area Wilderness, Summer 1996.

35   South Fork of the Shenandoah River, Virginia, just north of Bixler Bridge and Town of Luray, Summer 1997.

38   Bennett Rosenthal (foreground) and Kip Hurley at camp on the James River between Scottsville and Bremo Bluff, Summer 1995.

41   Kip Hurley and Sam Heller play at camp on Thompson's Island on the Allegheny River in Pennsylvania, Summer 1998.

42   Camp on Forked Lake in the Adirondacks, Summer 1998.

Index of Photographs

Page　*Caption*

43　Author and son Kip in camp on the James River, just above Bremo Bluff, Summer 1995. Photo by Michael Rosenthal.

47　Michael Rosenthal and daughter Emma in the "Trough" of the South Branch of the Potomac River in West Virginia, Summer 1999.

48　A swimmer's view of the Falls at Lac Chartier in La Verendrye Reserve, Quebec, Summer 1999.

49　Boatwright Tom Tompkins paddling freestyle in one of his Chemaun canoes on the Nottoway River in Virginia, Winter 1997.

52　Moose by the Boom House campsite on the South Branch of the Penobscot River in Maine, Summer 2002.

53　Otter on the South Branch of the Penobscot River in Maine, Summer 2002.

54　Robbie Fralick swings into the Peace River in Florida, Fall 1999.

56　Shoreline of Clark Lake in the Sylvania Wilderness, Upper Peninsula of Michigan, Summer 1999.

57　View from the High Bank camp on Chamberlain Lake on the Allagash Wilderness Waterway in Maine, Summer 1996.

61　End of the carry to Second Lake (Snowbank Lake region), in the Boundary Waters Canoe Area Wilderness, Summer 2003.

62　Caroline Hurley walks atop a beaver lodge on Rock Pond Outlet in the Adirondacks, Summer 2002.

64　Lunch stop on a grass island in the James River, between Scottsdale and Bremo Bluff, Virginia, Summer 1995.

66　The author cooking dinner on Lake Agnes in the Boundary Waters Canoe Area Wilderness, Summer 1998.

67　Biscuits baking in a campfire reflector oven.

70　Pine tree in the Congaree Swamp of South Carolina, Winter 1997.

Page *Caption*

73 Robin Lauer (stern) and Kip Hurley in a Chestnut Prospector, headed for Obabika Lake in the Temagami Canoe Country, Ontario, Summer 2000.

74 Kip Hurley and Robbie Fralick on the Peace River in Florida, Fall 1999.

78 Holeb Falls on the Moose River, in Maine, Summer 1998.

81 Falls at Lac Chartier in La Verendrye Reserve, Quebec, Summer 1999.

84 Grass on the St. Croix River in Maine, Summer 1999.

87 Allagash River in Maine, seen from Five Finger Brook campsite, Summer 1996.

90 Michael and Bennett Rosenthal on the Potomac River below Paw Paw, West Virginia, Summer 1997.

92 Author's canoe beached on Bear Island in North Carolina, Spring 1995.

93 John and Susan Ward lift their canoe over a beaver dam on the Oswegatchie River above High Falls, Spring 1997.

112 Canadian boy scouts on Lake Opeongo in Algonquin Provincial Park, Ontario, Summer 1997.

115 Julie (stern) and Caroline Hurley and "Jingles" on Raquette Lake in the Adirondacks, Summer 1998.

117 Caroline and Kip in their fort made of birch bark during rainy days camped on Forked Lake in the Adirondacks, Summer 1998.

118 Still waters of Chamberlain Lake in Maine near Lock Dam, at dawn, after two stormy days had prevented any passage on the lake, Summer 1996.

120 Canoes at the ready on Hay Lake, at the end of the portage from Glimmerglass Lake, in the Sylvania Wilderness of the Upper Peninsula of Michigan, Summer 1999.

122 Author and son Kip looking out from the second night's camp on the Delaware River in Pennsylvania, Spring 2000.

Index of Photographs

Page *Caption*

123   Julie (bow) and Kip Hurley paddle in a stiff breeze on
        Chesuncook Lake, Maine, Summer 2002.

126   Will Mistrot (foreground) and Kip Hurley diving for mussels in
        Temagami Canoe Country, Ontario, Summer 2000.

129   Caroline Claire Hurley, age 4, on the Pasquotank River in
        North Carolina, Fall 1996.

130   Big South Fork of the Cumberland River in Kentucky, Spring
        1999.

132   Big South Fork of the Cumberland River in Kentucky, Spring
        1999.

134   Author loading canoe on the Moose River in Maine, Summer
        1998.

135   Running Little Falls rapids on the St. Croix River in Maine,
        Summer 1999.

137   Another swimmer's view of the Falls at Lac Chartier in La
        Verendrye Reserve, Quebec, Summer 1999.

140   Kip Hurley and Robbie Fralick play in the Peace River, Fall
        1999

142   Robin Lauer and his Chestnut Canoe on Lac La Perche in La
        Verendrye Reserve, Quebec, Summer 1999.

144   John Ward overlooking the Bog River Flow near Low's Lake in
        the Adirondacks, Spring 1997.

145   Caroline, Julie and Kip Hurley on the beach in St. Augustine,
        Florida.

148   Author paddling on Lake Opeongo in Algonquin Provincial
        Park, Summer 1997.

150   Top: Camp on Green River in Mammoth Cave National Park,
        Kentucky, Spring 2002.

150   Bottom: Author cleaning fish caught on the Delaware River,
        Spring 2000.

152   Author in lean-to on "Fortyone" Island on Lac LaCroix in the
        Boundary Waters Canoe Area Wilderness, Summer 1998.

Page   *Caption*

154   Caroline Hurley walks a log by camp on Little Tupper Lake,
       Adirondacks, Summer 2002.

159   Will Mistrot (above) and Kip Hurley explore the stream
       between Small and Diamond Lakes in the Temagami Canoe
       Country of Ontario, Summer 2000.

162   Campers wait for a dawn paddle on Little Tupper Lake in the
       Adirondacks, Summer 2002.

165   Author stands atop Curtain Falls in the Boundary Waters
       Canoe Area Wilderness, Summer 1996. Photo by Brad
       Peacock.

168   Top: Kip Hurley hoists a smallmouth bass he caught on his own
       from camp on the Potomac River, Summer 1997.

168   Bottom: Author with northern pike taken on Grand Lac
       Victoria, in La Verendrye Reserve, Quebec, Summer 1999.

170   Tom Tompkins walks a shallow spot in the South Fork of the
       Shenandoah River, Virginia, Summer 1997.

171   Catch of the day on Iron Lake in the Boundary Waters Canoe
       Area Wilderness, Summer 1996.

174   Top: The author's great uncle, Monnie LaCroix, with wife
       Lucille and friend at their farm in Tennessee, Summer 1973.

174   Bottom: The author's great uncle, Jefferson Davis LaCroix, at
       home in Puryear Hollow, near Pulaski, Tennessee, Summer
       1973.

175   Kip Hurley (river and date unknown).

176   Nesting loon on Lake Opeongo in Algonquin Provincial Park,
       Quebec, Summer 1997.

178   Brad Peacock makes ready on Crooked Lake after the portage
       around Curtain Falls, Summer 1996.

180   Falls on Little Indian Sioux River in the Boundary Waters
       Canoe Area Wilderness, Summer 1998.

181   Moose calf on the Allagash River in Maine, Summer 1996.

182   Author beside Allagash Falls in Maine, Summer 1996. Photo
       by Michael Rosenthal.

Index of Photographs

Page   *Caption*

184   Mike Avery paddles the Tyger River in South Carolina as Caroline Hurley fishes for leaves, Summer 1998.

187   Canoes wait at author's camp on Forked Lake, Summer 1998.

188   Caroline Hurley reads another "Harry Potter" novel while Dad paddles on the South Branch of the Penobscot River in Maine, Summer 2002.

192   Campsite on Lake Opeongo in Algonquin Provincial Park, Quebec, Summer 1997.

193   Party on the Big South Fork of the Cumberland River in Kentucky nearly swamps their canoe coming over a ledge, Spring 1999.

195   Caroline Hurley (foreground) and pals on the Tyger River in South Carolina, Summer 1998.

196   Author in camp on the Delaware River, Spring 2000.

198   Dr. Mark Heller emerges from the tent on an island of the Allegheny River in Pennsylvania, Summer 1998.

201   Kip Hurley and "Jingles" in the Congaree Swamp National Forest, Winter 1997.

204   Author and son Kip camped on the Edisto River in South Carolina, Spring 2001.

205   Kip Hurley and his first pike, taken on the Riviere de la Baie, in La Verendrye Reserve, Quebec, Summer 1999.

206   Caroline Hurley inspecting water lilies on Rock Pond Outlet in the Adirondacks, Summer 2002.

207   Kip Hurley and "Jingles" with a bluegill on the James River, Virginia, Summer 1995.

209   Couple carrying over beaver dam in Rock Pond Outlet in the Adirondacks, Summer 2002.

212   Author's camp on Polliwog Pond in the Adirondacks, Summer 1995.

213   Slickrock Creek falls at the outlet to Cheoah Lake, Great Smoky Mountains, Spring 2002.

Page   *Caption*

215   Scene at dusk on an unnamed brook near Grass Pond on Low's Lake, in the Adirondacks, Spring 1997.

216   Canoeists on the Moose River in Maine, Summer 1998.

218   Canoes at the ready at the foot of Allagash Falls in Maine, Summer 1996.

220   Julie, Kip and Caroline with the family's trusty Jeep on Ocracoke Island.